The Book On

JOY

*May you joyful moments
multiply.*

Robn Eldridge Hau

JAN FRASER INSPIRED LIFE SERIES

The Book On

JOY

WRITTEN BY
30 Heart-Centered Phenomenal Women Authors

Foreword by Jack Canfield, co-creator of Chicken Soup for the Soul® and co-author of The Success Principles™

First Edition

Copyright ©2021 Jan Fraser Inspired Life Series
www.janfraser.com

ISBN: 978-0-9801104-4-9

Acknowledgements
Book Designer: Sue Luehring | sjldesign.carbonmade.com
Website designer: AndreavaKasianchuk | createandfulfillconsulting.com

www.thebookonjoy.com

We dedicate this book to you . . . our sisters, friends, mothers, aunts, grandmothers, teachers, leaders and all the women who light the world daily with Joy. In this, we honor the many women who have gone before us, lighting our path and teaching us the quality of Joy.

No matter your circumstance, your country, your story, we walk alongside you in the search for more joy in your life and the world.

Enjoy your Joy Journeys . . .

CONTRIBUTING AUTHORS

Barbara Blue
Paddy Briggs
Nancy Carlson
Victoria Chadderton
Ilka V. Chavez
Dr. Alice Cheung
Rev. Gayle Dillon
Ann Smith Gordon, R.N., MBE
Lorna Granger
Robin E. Hain
Trisha Jacobson
Andreava Kasianchuk
Fauzia Khan
Lila M. Larson
Maria Elena Laufs

Dr. Mori Morris-Mitchell
Diane Palmer
Starr Pilmore, R.N.
Debbie Prinster
Bernadette Ridge
Jennie Ritchie
Grace Rosales
Sakshi Salve
Angela I. Schutz
Kristin Sparks
Su Stacey
Cindy Stewart, R.N.
Cherylanne Thomas
Ilya Vita
Jane Williams

Reprinted with Permissions

TABLE OF CONTENTS

Sharing Joy

Invitation

INTRODUCTION

The Book on Joy was the result of inspiration meeting action.

Last December, while on a zoom call with my writer retreat participants, I related a tiny experience where joy was the result. I was at the local post office with a long line of waiting customers and no movement toward the agent's position. Everything was stalled and the time was speeding toward 5pm and closing.

I knew it would be a long wait and I didn't trust myself to mail it at the self-service kiosk where no one was waiting in line. I had committed to a coaching client at a certain time and was nervous that I would be late. Just then, a young man in line ahead of me noticed that I had my eye focused on the self-serve parcel station wishing I had the experience to try it and lose my place in line.

He kindly signaled for me to come over to the self-serve station and helped me weigh and mail my parcel with the right postage. He was not a postal employee. He was a customer like me. And yet, he took the time, got out of line and cared to help me send my package even though he was still in the longer line waiting for the agent's help.

I was overcome with gratitude. It was the Christmas season, postal crunch time and I was not expecting anyone's help, certainly not another customer's. I thanked him and offered a reward but he refused it, wishing me a very Happy Holiday.

It was a joyful experience!

It stayed on my mind and I related the experience when on the zoom call with my writers. Inspiration made me say, "We need more Joy in the world like the experience at the post office." Wouldn't we have a more beautiful, kind, loving world if everyone felt more joy and helped others feel it too.

That is how *The Book on Joy* was born.

The book is designed in four sections: Finding Joy, Choosing Joy, Living Joy and Sharing Joy. The stories and content of all the 30 heart-centered phenomenal women authors are original and authentic. When they share their journeys to joy in their own words, they are speaking to you. Their purpose is to inspire you to engage more with joy and make it a conscious part of your daily life.

The Book on Joy is the first volume in the Inspired Life Series. In each of the forthcoming books, we will assist, support and suggest ways that you could live a more inspired life. This is only the beginning . . .

Joy is a daily divine experience to be discovered, celebrated and shared. If you would like to experience the essential oil called Joy to put on your heart each morning before you start your day, reach out to me at info@janfraser.com and our team will send you a free sample.

With this book as your inspiration, may we all live with more joy in our lives and wrap the world in 'joy-ness.'

Welcome to our Inspired Life Series Community!

Love and Joy,

Jan

Jack Canfield

Jack Canfield, known as America's #1 Success Coach, is a bestselling author, professional speaker, trainer, and entrepreneur. He is the founder and CEO of the Canfield Training Group, which trains entrepreneurs, educators, corporate leaders and motivated individuals how to accelerate the achievement of their personal and professional goals.

He has conducted live trainings for more than a million people in more than 50 countries around the world. He holds two Guinness World Record titles and is a member of the National Speakers Association's Speaker Hall of Fame.

Jack is the coauthor of more than two hundred books, including, T*he Success Principles™: How to Get from Where You Are to Where You Want to Be, The Success Principles Workbook,* and the *Chicken Soup for the Soul®* series, which includes forty New York Times bestsellers and has sold more than 500 million copies in 47 languages around the world.

Jack is a featured teacher in the movie *The Secret,* and has appeared on more than a thousand radio and television shows, including *The Oprah Winfrey Show, Oprah's Super Soul Sunday, the Today show, Fox & Friends,* and *Larry King Live.*

Foreword

By Jack Canfield

Co-Creator of the best-selling *Chicken Soup for the Soul®* series
Co-Author of *The Success Principles*™

L ove, Joy and Gratitude are the three most important emotional states for living a happy, successful and abundant life. You now hold in your hands a powerful tool to help you expand your experience of joy.

In my work with the law of attraction, I know how powerful joy can be to helping people manifest what they want in their lives. I am continually telling my students, trainers and speaking audience members that the more they focus on creating and embracing joy, the easier their lives will get.

When Jan approached me to write the foreword for *The Book on Joy©*, I instantly said yes for three reasons.

First, I believe we need to create more joy in our world. Over the last 50 years as a motivational and inspirational speaker and transformational trainer, I have emphasized the need to maintain a high vibration state of joy while keeping one's dreams and goals in sight. Joy is a critical aspect of achieving those dreams and goals, because as we focus on living in a state of joy, we attract more things to be joyful about.

And because of all the challenges we face in our current world, joy is most needed at this time in our lives. As you'll discover, joy is contagious. It lifts up others — our families, our friends and ultimately our larger communities — when we are in a state of joy. Along with love, joy has the power to relax, heal, soothe, and comfort us.

After a lifetime of intentionally choosing, creating, and embracing joy, I have been rewarded in so many ways — with wealth, health, great relationships, meaningful impact, and professional fulfillment.

There are many ways to create joy in our lives including spending time with high vibration people, meditating, repeating positive affirmations, listening to uplifting music, dancing, doing things you love to do (playing ping pong with my wife is my latest favorite), exercise and laughing, just to name a few. Another thing that I have added lately is the daily practice of applying Young Living's blend called JOY over my heart. I do this every morning, and since I have started this practice, I have noticed a palpable difference in maintaining that steady experience of joy.

Second, Jan has gathered together in this book women whose lives resonate with joy and encouraged them to share their heartfelt messages within these pages. The 30 heart-centered authors of this book are all graduates of my Breakthrough to Success and Train the Trainer programs and are the heart of this book. They know that the magic ingredient in life and healing is joy. From eight different countries they span the globe in their messages of how to move through life facing challenges and making it through by drawing upon the light of joy.

These 30 women are speakers, trainers, coaches, counselors, mentors with challenges on both the home and professional fronts while always maintaining a joyful attitude in the face of those challenges. I know the insights and wisdom they offer in this book will inspire you and countless other women.

Third, the stories are all true and uplifting. Having co-authored more than 200 *Chicken Soup for the Soul*® books, which are read all around the world, bringing hope, courage, inspiration, and love to millions of people, I know how these types of stories of hope, triumph, and resiliency are an unquestionably powerful tool in transforming people's lives. I encourage you to allow the stories in this book to touch you deeply and change your life.

The Book on Joy® is a veritable feast for women who may have given up on feeling joy or who have put their lives on hold or lost sight of their dreams — or for anyone who would like to feel a little more joy. No matter how small or how large your current challenges are, reading this book will help you find more joy as you face life's challenges. ❀

Jan Fraser

❁

Jan is a 'self-starter', bringing real world customer service experience to her keynotes, training and coaching. An airline industry superstar, she rose from the ramp support team to instructor, training thousands of flight attendants.

Jan was a Seminar Speaker for Skill Path and National Seminars, and Adjunct Professor at Bermuda College. She is a Success and Writing Coach and traveled the world to deliver training in the US and seven countries.

Jan is a sought after Keynote Speaker. She is the author of seven books and coaches writers through virtual and onsite retreats. She co-created Success University for Women best sellers and is the Creator of the Jan Fraser Inspired Life Series.

She has a CSP® (Certified Speaking Professional™) designation from the National Speakers Association.

Jan lives with her husband in Lake Las Vegas and Bermuda, balancing her life between two shores.

Contact

Website: www.janfraser.com
Email: jan@janfraser.com

Live Your Inspired Life

By Jan Fraser

"Know what sparks the light in you, so that you, in your own way, can illuminate the world."

— Oprah

Welcome to our "Inspired Life Series" of books and this volume: *The Book on Joy.*

Definitions state it is the emotion of great delight or happiness caused by something exceptionally good or satisfying. That is descriptive. Yet, the real experience of joy is freeing and exhilarating with an extra opportunity for gusto.

It makes a heart feel warm and happy.

No matter whether you have experienced Joy in your youth or your maturity, it is a life-affirming experience that everyone deserves, now more than ever, with the challenges that we face daily.

I believe in joy and joyful experiences. I always have.

From earliest memories to this day, joy gets my attention and gives my heart and soul a soothing balm of protection against any wrinkles (upsets) in the landscape of my day.

When I was a toddler and discovered crayons, I used the purple one to draw a picture on my parents' new beige Samsonite hard-sided luggage. I was joyful as I expanded my artistic talent on that suitcase, my new canvas for artwork. My father was not happy and I received a spanking. I was in the midst of joy. Dad was into discipline. Strangely enough, though memorable, that spanking did not dim my joy. Why? I knew I was loved or that I had experienced joy prior to the spanking so I knew it was possible to have again. I dried my tears and recovered. A life with joy would continue and it did.

With my sister, I visited my aunt and uncle for a week in Canton, Ohio once a year. It was the highlight of the summer as they lived a long drive from us in an immense two-story home. After dinner one night, I ventured to the neighboring park behind their house and encountered a beautiful, tall Irish setter. I had never seen one before as our Friskie was a tiny cocker spaniel mix from the dog pound. I was drawn to the red fur with delighted exuberance. When I reached out to pet the setter, I didn't notice she was eating her dinner and the joy of petting her became a shocking experience when she bit my upper arm. Bleeding and crying, I walked slowly back to my uncle's home and we immediately left for the emergency department of the local hospital. There was pain and sadness involved as I was forbidden to swim in Meyer's Lake with my cousins due to the bandages and possible infection. Regardless of being bitten that summer, the intense joy of loving and owning dogs has continued my entire life.

I've learned that joy will shine through the most challenging situations if you look for it and are open to it. In my adult life, I have had issues that have clouded my joy temporarily, such as divorces, disappointments, setbacks, discriminations, critics, offenses, etc. You may have experienced these challenges and others. Some of these happen to every human . . . no one escapes completely . . . but what are we doing about them? Do we find the joy, somehow, in some way?

When my father died on my birthday, October 4th, I was in shock and grief. I asked him in spirit, "Why, Dad, why did you leave me on my birthday?" It was my favorite day of the year. I even had an email address back then: jan@10-4.com.

It was difficult. In response to Dad's passing, two of my friends reached out to me with completely opposite messages.

One friend, Judy said, "I heard your father passed away and with your mother gone, too, you're an orphan now!" That statement was hard to take at that moment of grieving. I refuted it.

I explained, "I had parents and now their gone, that doesn't make me an orphan!"

My second friend, Diane, said, "I heard your father passed away on your birthday and you're having a tough time. He is sending you a message of love. You took him into your home and nursed him for the last few years of his life. He chose to leave the planet on your birthday to send you a message of love and thanks because he was unable to speak his message."

I immediately relaxed and breathed deeply.

I found joy in Diane's message and preferred to dwell on that. It was as if, her words allowed the veil of sadness to part and the sun to come out for a few minutes.

That year, I started a new birthday practice. Now, on October 4th each year, I celebrate Dad's life (his gifts of family love and devotion, military and government service in World War II and beyond) on my birthday. He is in spirit with me on that day and while I have feet on the ground, he is in my heart and together we celebrate his life and my birthday on the same day.

These situations may sound familiar to you and you may be able to relate to some of these events. We're all in this life together.

"The walls we build around us to keep sadness out also keeps out the joy." —Jim Rohn

I have found there is usually a tiny grain of joy somewhere in every life event.

For me, finding joy on October 4th is a choice. Seeking and finding joy requires intentionality. We have to search for it sometimes and we will find it. You can find joy in tiny events; they don't have to be huge.

Recently, I was sharing about The Book on Joy with a woman in her 50's. I invited her to participate and she replied, "I'm not sure that I've experienced joy." That surprised me, so I tried to ask more questions to trigger some ideas — ways that she might have felt joy in some way and did not realize it. I asked her if she had someone special in her life, or if she had a hobby — it turned out she did and she realized that she found joy in that pursuit. In fact, after our conversation, she recognized that she actually did have joy in a few areas of her life. Often we may have felt joy at some point, but perhaps didn't recognize it as such. If you're living in a cloud, you may have joy in your life, but not be able to see it.

Stay aware and cognizant and look for your joy.

If you are someone who has been beaten down or led to believe that you are not deserving or worthy of joy, that's a lie. Joy is not only for certain people; it is for all people. You are absolutely worthy and deserving of joy just as you are. Believe that it is out there or in there for you.

If you were not taught how to see joy if it's not a habit for you . . . it's not too late to find it. Know that it is a worthy pursuit, not a frivolous one.

Maybe you were taught about joy but have since lost the ability to notice it or your life experiences have tamped it down.

Perhaps you're a seasoned joy receiver, finding it easier to recognize. Even then, you may need joy "jogs" now and then to remember.

No matter which of these you can relate to, the more you embrace joy, the more joy you will find.

Here are my personal "Joy Gems" to jumpstart your joy journey:

1. Count Your Blessings . . . we forget to do this and it needs to be a daily practice.
2. Live in the present moment . . . concentrate on your breathing for a few minutes and treasure that experience.
3. Stay connected to a tribe, family, a community...join our Joy Community and keep joy in your heart and on your heart daily each morning.
4. Shower others with kindness . . . be aware of how you can be helpful to others.
5. Focus on self-care . . . be good to yourself.
6. Exercise . . . walk, move, do something.
7. Let go of blaming, shaming or complaining.
8. Use Essential Oils to Reset any challenges in your life and your day. Do a reset daily and use your essential oils, AFT.

Whether you are experienced at finding and embracing joy, or whether it's something you've been searching for, this book can help you.

Start today. Start with these stories to learn how to find, choose, live and share joy. Build the foundation of joy in your life.

Use this book as a springboard, a referral. This book is a cozy blanket you can use to wrap yourself up during difficult times, and get back in the 'joy stream' of life.

Keep it close whenever you feel like there is no joy for you...simply jump into this book and its magical pages will adjust your vision and your heart.

May you have countless joyful days, years and lifetimes yet to be discovered . . . 🏵

JAN FRASER INSPIRED LIFE SERIES

Finding

JOY

Maria Elena Laufs

Maria Elena Laufs is a lecturer at the University of Duisburg-Essen and the University of Applied Sciences in Düsseldorf, Germany. She also enjoys running regular motivational workshops for women. Her aim is to inspire them to first define and then go and live the lives they truly desire. She believes that finding your joy in life is the key to unlocking this, and this is what drew her to this book.

As a former executive in the world of international fashion retailing and buying, she is highly skilled in intercultural communication and teamwork. Having lived and worked in a variety of countries, she is also well-versed in the challenges facing globally mobile women.

When not teaching or training, you'll find her attempting to master yoga poses, surfing clothing websites keeping abreast of the latest trends, or trying to keep up with her husband as they explore Germany by bicycle. All done in a spirit of joy, of course.

Contact
Website: www.mariaelenalaufs.com
Email: info@mariaelenalaufs.com

Building a Backbone

By Maria Elena Laufs

"The joy we have has little to do with the circumstances of our lives and everything to do with the focus of our lives"

— Russell M. Nelson

I grew up in a castle in the middle of the glorious British countryside. When I say a castle, I mean a grand fairy tale castle with 356 rooms on top of a hill, complete with towers, turrets and splendid peacocks roaming the manicured grounds. You may now be thinking that I am a blue-blooded member of the aristocracy, but nothing could be further from the truth. I am the daughter of Spanish immigrants who were the live-in chefs for the then Duke and Duchess. My story is more Cinderella than Sleeping Beauty.

Despite the enchanting surroundings and being part of a loving, typically Spanish family, it was a rather lonely existence for a child. My parents worked long hours and the magnificent isolation of my home wasn't exactly conducive to meeting other children and making friends. In retrospect, this was when I first started to actively focus on finding joy in my life. When I talk about joy, I'm talking about the lift that comes from absolute, pure contentment. This I found by invisibly and unobtrusively entering the two fascinating, magical worlds that surrounded me. The one being that of the adult servants, and the other the glamourous, intriguing world of the British upper class. A plethora of people are needed to run a castle, providing me with an inexhaustible supply of staff to surreptitiously hang around. My bank of joyous, lasting memories accumulated and included cleaning the hundreds of swords in the guard's room, stacking the crisply laundered bedding in the cavernous cupboard, preparations for the grand weekend shooting parties, and, together with my father, plucking the resulting dozens of pheasants. Adding to this was the tantalising glimpse into the world of the aristocracy where, to my awestruck eyes, all the women were beautiful and wonderfully stylish. My greatest admiration however was saved for the Duchess herself, who would stride around the castle looking fabulous, always wearing bright pink lipstick and leaving a trail of perfume in her wake. This is undoubtedly where my interest in beauty and fashion was sparked. Doing the rounds with the housekeeper, I would spy copies of Vogue magazine lying around, take mental note of the lotions and potions adorning the ornate dressing tables and gaze admiringly at the exquisite designer outfits hanging casually in the bedrooms.

In my world, everything was glorious, however, when I was nine years old, my father committed suicide after suffering a nervous breakdown. My memories of my father are generally good ones, and I was too young to be aware of the depth of his private anguish. This event triggered a new phase in my life and the revelation of new sources of joy. My two-year-old brother suffered from a medical condition requiring him to take medication daily to prevent convulsions, a duty that fell to me. This awakened the joy of having responsibility. Then I made a friend who became my partner-in-crime in my magical castle life, spending countless joyful hours together exploring the labyrinth of passageways in our fantasy world. The huge, centuries-old castle walls provided me with the perfect spot to nurture the glee in executing an accurate tennis shot, an activity that occupied me for innumerable hours. Unbeknown to me at the time, the fundamentals of my "Joy Backbone" had been constructed and consisted of, a nicely decorated home, stylish clothes, a friend, tennis, and responsibility. Then, after 18 happy years in the idyllic countryside, city life beckoned, and I set off to explore London and the delights of university life.

London offered a myriad of opportunities and I enthusiastically set about taking full advantage of them. Shopping at Harrods and Selfridges, clubbing at Camden Palace and the Hippodrome, seeing West End plays and going to Wimbledon to see the tennis. It was the mid-eighties, and I was having the time of my life being in the big city, sporting big hair, and even bigger shoulder pads. Happily, I also managed to do enough work to successfully complete my Business Studies degree. This ushered in the era of my life where most of my jumping-for-joy moments stemmed from achievement and accomplishment in my career. Following my love of fashion, I was working in the retail apparel industry and had immediately been captivated by the power of clothing and how to help people look good. The downside of this fantastic job was the obligation to move locations every few years to take up new positions and promotions, uprooting my life on a regular basis. The work part was a consistent source of joy, but I needed to replicate that emotion outside of work. At 24, I was transferred to a small town in the UK I had never heard of, let alone knew where it was. Echoes of the isolation of my castle days had started to appear, so I decided to take matters into my own hands and deliberately focus on bringing joy into my life.

My "Joy Backbone," which had been passively in the background for years, came to fruition and took centre stage in my plan. One day after work, I sat alone in my hotel room and reviewed my life so far. Honing in on the moments when I had felt most joyous, I wrote a list and this served as my platform for future joyous moments, whatever my circumstances may be. My list comprised of a nice home, fitness classes (the 80s aerobics craze had not bypassed me), tennis, Spanish practice and a friend to hang out with. Taking immediate action, I found fitness classes, signed up for Spanish classes and killed two birds with one stone by finding somewhere nice to live and a friend for the weekends in the same place. This deliberate focus on the roots of my joy served me well five times more as I was relocated the length and breadth of the country. After twelve years climbing the career ladder, I landed the job of my dreams working as a fashion buyer, which provided me with a non-stop smorgasbord of joy. Life couldn't get any better. I had a beautiful home in a converted manor (the closest I could get to a castle), was spending time with my friends, travelling all over the world for work, meeting new people and experiencing new cultures. Then, out of nowhere, at the age of 37, I was struck by Cupid's arrow.

Prince Charming appeared in my life in the guise of a widowed American living in Germany who was a work colleague. He was the father of three children under the age of ten who couldn't speak a word of English. At the time, I was living in the UK and my knowledge of German was limited to *bier garden* and *schnitzel*. Within a year, I had swapped my high-flying career girl lifestyle for a new role as a stay-at-home housewife in a small German town. To say this was a shock to the system would be an understatement. The elation of being married to the love of my life was severely challenged by the limited day-to-day joy I was experiencing. My husband worked long hours, my family and friends were all in another country and I was now a mother to three children I could only communicate with using sign language and exaggerated expressions. Looking back, it was comical, but at the time it was less so. My "Joy Backbone" had been forgotten in the whirlwind of my new life, and I decided it was time to resurrect it. Having been abruptly thrust into the world of motherhood, I now found time to myself severely limited. Children only attend school in the morning in Germany, meaning I had a precious four-hour window of opportunity every day. The first thing I worked on was decorating my new home. The house I was living in bore no reflection of my tastes, so I started with the curtains. This had always been my starting point and my aim was to mimic the opulent castle-like drapes I had grown up with. Alongside this, I joined a sports club, found an English friend and threw myself wholeheartedly into German lessons. This was when *learning something new* made it onto my "Joy Backbone." Accomplishment now took the form of such things as successfully navigating parents' evening and following the instructions during German yoga classes whilst head down in *downward-facing dog*. After three enlightening years in Germany, my husband was offered a new job with his company. We packed our bags and moved to Hong Kong.

Hong Kong is an amazing place, and it was love at first sight. Living on the other side of the world offered a dazzling array of new places to explore, cultures to experience, people to meet and things to learn. With the boys being at an all-day school, together with the luxury of having a live-in helper, I suddenly found myself in the enviable position of not actually having anything to do. I had become a duchess myself and, instead of a castle on top of a hill, I was living in a luxurious duplex pent-house apartment overlooking the splendour of the South China Sea. All of the elements of my "Joy Backbone" were firmly in place, except one, responsibility. After mastering the fundamentals of Mah-jong and learn-ing enough basic Cantonese to navigate the local mini-buses, the time had come to learn something that would fill the responsibility void and enable me to have more purpose. It was time to seize the opportunity to do something I had had my eye on for a while and become an English as a Second Language teacher. During my untold hours as a student in Ger-man classes, I had always rather fancied leading the classes and now I had the chance to do so. Within a couple of months, I found myself chalk in hand, in front of 35 schoolchildren all wearing pristine white uniforms and looking at me with a mixture of curiosity and expectation. It was a real baptism of fire. This teaching experience gave me an *opportunity to motivate and give confidence* to my "Joy Backbone." I had discovered the fundamental thread between my earlier joy derived from giving people confidence through their clothes, and this new joy which came to me from giving students confidence through their speaking abilities. After four wonderful years teaching and living in Hong Kong, my husband's job took us back to Germany.

November doesn't showcase Germany at its best. The days are dark, chilly and short. It's that limbo period before the whole country lights up and becomes the magical place of bustling Christmas markets, fragrant *Glühwein*, and mystical *nutcrackers*. Arriving at this time of year, I wasn't exactly feeling most joyous. It was cold, my English friend had left for Singapore, we were living in temporary accommodations, and I hadn't hit a tennis ball in months. Devoid of my "Joy Backbone" and languishing on the sofa one day, I finally gathered my focus and determination reinstall-ing my "Joy Backbone" and making it stronger.

Ten years later, my life couldn't be better. All the elements of my "Joy Backbone" which have become evident during these years are present. These include my remodelled home, complete with opulent curtains, uplifting, supportive friends and plenty of tennis. I have two fulfilling jobs that both provide me with the opportunity to motivate and inspire confidence; lecturing at two local universities and running motivational workshops for women.

Matured from my Cinderella years, I now aim to be a Fairy Godmother. In place of a magic wand, I have my "Joy Backbone."

You have one too. Have you seen yours lately?

Notes

Barbara Blue

❀

Barbara lives on The Wild Atlantic Way, in Connemara, Co Galway, Ireland. She lives with her daughter DeAnna. Both are native Gaelic speakers, something which is only still common in a few small pockets of Ireland called a 'Gaeltacht'.

Barbara has a BA Hons degree in English and Irish, from NUIG College, Ireland. After college she spent a few years in Milwaukee, US, and when she returned to Ireland she somehow found herself working in the world of accountancy and finance. She went on to do an online Diploma in Psychology and Counselling — probably to delve deeper into how she ended up working as an accountant! In order to remind herself of the 'inner author' she hoped was still lurking within, Barbara spent a few years writing scripts for a long-running Irish speaking (Gaelic) soap drama called Ros na Run, on top of her full-time finance job.

When Barbara is not avidly reading as many books as she can, she loves to cook, watch movies, and partake in just 'one or two' glasses of wine...since all bottles are made of glass after all . . .

Contact
Email: babsblue@gmail.com

A Light at the End of all Tunnels

By Barbara Blue

"Don't add days to your life, add life to your days"

— Anonymous

Sometimes, life can feel like a long road of trials and tribulations. Of drudgery, loss, grief, sorrow, struggles, and anxiety. It can be easy to fall into the pattern of just trudging through each day, in monotonous repetition. Living like this can lead to feelings of resentment, bitterness, sadness, and inadequacy. We spend too much time regretting things in the past, or anxious and stressing about what might happen in the future. When we get wrapped up in these habits, we start to cloud our own opportunities to see the joy in life.... but it is there, just waiting for us to find it! We can look for it in the big exuberant times of our lives, and can also find it in the more mundane everyday activities, once we know how to appreciate and acknowledge it.

I am a 45 year old single-mother, who has dealt with a variety of personal struggles over the years — emotionally, physically, and financially. I have had a failed marriage, and subsequent failed relationships since then. I have endured physical and mental abuse in some of those. I have never had much financial wealth, and have always had to rely on tight budgets to see me through. I have endured the death of my mother and my brother, as well as other loved ones along the way. I have various medical issues that are the cause of almost daily pain or discomfort. These are all different things that have dragged me down to the darkest places over the years. I have felt like no matter how hard I try, I keep hitting brick walls to push me back again to the dim corners, where misery and self-doubt reside. I still have those feelings.

Thankfully, I have gotten better at being able to find joy. It is a learning curve, and one that I feel needs to be practised, in order to filter through the silt of hardship and the self-applied layers of anxiety that I am continuously striving to peel away.

Being a single mom for over 20 years has definitely brought its own hardships. However, I have found great joy in seeing my daughter grow from toddler to teenager and into an intelligent and beautiful collegiate woman. This has given me so much more joy than I can adequately put into words. When times were tough and finances were particularly low, she taught me the value of adding life to our days in ways that cost us nothing. By doing things like building a camping fort in our sitting room and pretending it was a 'different land' we found laughter, joy and connection. We could read, draw, picnic together and find ways to feel genuine joy and love and contentment. When stress and worry would start to prevail, she would be able to chase it away with a kiss and a hug, and a giggle. It's a gift she still has and bestows on me regularly — the way to lift my heart and make me smile when I most need it!

We are currently going through a global pandemic, and Ireland had level 5 lockdown restrictions in place for a long time. For months on end, we were not allowed to travel outside a 5km radius unless for essential purposes. All shops, cinemas, restaurants, pubs, and more were closed, except for shops selling vital items such as groceries. We were instructed not to mix with other households. Covid 19 may have taken some of our loved ones away from us, but so has mental health issues with people who found the isolation too much to bear. It has been a tough road. My daughter and I have supported each other through this and have found laughter and joy in simple things like a game of Scrabble or cards, watching a good movie, or sometimes dancing around our kitchen like lunatics with a glass of wine in hand! Constantly worrying about when this pandemic might end, and 'how many days' we have to wait until that happens, will only make the time feel longer. However, adding life and laughter and joy to our days has helped ease the process in so many ways.

When my mother died from emphysema in March 2011, life as I knew it shifted. I believed I had hit the deepest level of grief imaginable. The loss of her comforting presence, love and support, was almost too much to bear. And yet, even in those dark times, we were able to find joy in hearing stories from those who came to her funeral. They told us of a woman who, although she taught over 40 children a day as a teacher, and came home to raise seven of her own, still managed to find the time to help everyone in need. I learnt that she had cut up her wedding dress and sewed communion dresses for some children of the parish, who couldn't afford their own. She baked cakes, knitted and sewed items, and provided what she could to help others, even with as little personal time as she had left between her teaching and raising us. She brought so much joy to others. Hearing these stories helped us find joy in her loving and helpful nature.

Though it was a sad time to see Mom suffering in and out of hospital all the time before she died, there was joy in seeing how much my father loved her. Without knowing how many days she would have left with us, he added life to her days by spending each day with her — whether in hospital or at home. He would hold her hand, and they would speak for hours or sit in companionable silence. Their love for each other was unconditional, and right up to her burial it was beyond heart-warming to hear my Dad declare her 'always so beautiful.' They found their own joy in each other and gave us joy allowing us to witness their deep devotion. We were privileged to be the beneficiaries of their love and joy.

When my brother died by suicide in May 2014, I realised that there were deeper plains of grief after all, than what we had felt after losing my mother. The heavy dark shutters of grief clanged together so tightly at that time, not even a glimmer of light could infiltrate successfully. Here and there we could smile and laugh at his memory, but it felt like cold comfort in the face of the utter despair his loss had left behind. Finding joy at that time was a very hard task. However, being the funny, up-for-a-laugh, great guy that he was, it was only natural that his legacy of a lifetime of happy wonderful memories would eventually shine through. Little by little, our laughter became a little less broken as we recounted some of the mad-cap antics he would get up to. Once the laughter started settling more comfortably and began to feel less stilted, I realised that recounting such memories brought more and more joy each time. The grief and the empty spot he had left in our hearts and souls may never fill up completely. The sharp edges of sadness have dulled and have receded enough to show that joy in his memory doesn't have to hurt so much anymore. He was a man who knew how to add life to his days, as well as to the days of those around him. It is only fitting that his vivacity and sense of humour lives on to bring us joy.... though he had lost his own joy and sadly felt unable to add further days to his life.

The thing about finding joy is, that it truly does add life to your days.

Be it the joy of going for a walk with your best friend, with whom you can share everything, or dancing around with your daughter, or just having a quiet time to yourself while reading a good book. Events in life don't all have to be huge or astounding or boisterous in order to find joy, or to make your days more lively. None of us know how many days we can add to our lives, or even have left to us. Some of us may work on preserving our bodies cautiously, through careful diet and exercise. Some of us may overindulge in things that are not so healthy for us. With either path, there are still no actual guarantees of a longer or more fulfilling life.

But one thing we can focus more on, is having as full and joyful life as we can, while we are here. For some, this might mean grand-scale accomplishments such as climbing Mount Everest or raising a family (be it children, fur-babies, or even plants that you nurture or consider 'family'), or finding a career that you love, or a myriad of different things. As with any path of life, there can be bumps and setbacks, but it doesn't mean the path can't continue once you pass those hurdles.

There is no set 'game plan' for finding joy, as it is a concept and emotion as variable to each individual, as each individual is to each other. But it's a journey everyone should participate in, with many rewards.

Stop worrying about adding those days to your life, and instead start to add life to your days. Create those memories you want to treasure forever, go on the adventures you've dreamt about, and make the most of the journey of Finding Joy! 🏵️

Notes

Fauzia Khan

❀

Fauzia developed a 25-year career in the finance and software industries, where she earned accolades for leading her team and was on the fast-track as a rising executive. However, the path she thought would lead to happiness caused her to lose herself in a toxic marriage and difficult divorce.

Her divorce served as the catalyst to the path of redefining and rediscovering herself. She immersed herself in learning and reclaimed her self-identity. She found hope and built a practice based upon inner strength and outer support. She discovered the key to moving through adversity is to recognize you are not alone.

Today Fauzia is an entrepreneur with experience in retail, supply chain management and online sales. Her coaching and consulting services are based on struggles rebuilding her own life from divorce both personally and professionally. Fauzia helps clients explore their emotions, overcome shame, reclaim their power, and become better than before.

Contact

Website: www.findyoursparkduringdivorce.com
Email: fkhan@sparkupjoy.com

Finding My Joy During Divorce

By Fauzia Khan

"Your success and happiness lies in you. Resolve to keep happy, and your joy and you shall form an invincible host against difficulties."

— Helen Keller

On a harsh day in November, my life crashed as my husband told me he needed space to figure out his life. I was shocked. He had met someone else. I had hoped it was a brief midlife crisis though, I was embarrassed and disappointed when I found out it was not. I felt alone and paralyzed with shame that I couldn't share with anyone. This rejection led to depression and anxiety. I felt lost and unsure. After three months, I finally told my immediate family about my marriage failing.

At the age of 45, I left a successful career in the financial industry to start a new life with my husband. Our marriage expanded as business opportunities developed. As a spouse and business partner, I led four different companies ranging from property management to transportation logistics. My marriage became my priority which left little time for hobbies, friends, or even my family. All of my dreams came true with this financial success. I lived in my dream home, drove my dream car, traveled frequently, and could work from anywhere in the world.

I did not realize at the time, that I was not alone in my divorce journey. Fifteen percent of adult women in the United States are divorced compared to less than one percent in 1920. Almost 50 percent of all marriages in the U.S. end in separation or divorce — with a divorce occurring every 13 seconds. While divorce is declining for younger couples (ages 25 – 39), it is climbing for mature married folks. Studies from the Pew Research Center indicate the divorce rate for adults ages 50 and older doubled since the 1990s (2017). The rate increases for people like me who are married for less than 10 years (21 people per 1,000 married persons in 2015) in a first marriage compared to my husband who was in his second or multiple marriages (60%).

Though our marriage failed, I hoped for an amicable divorce since our relationship was entangled in several businesses. Financial insecurity after divorce is a real and reasonable fear. Like many women experiencing divorce at midlife, I no longer had a job. We expected to continue working together as we jointly owned three companies and my income was dependent on a company he created prior to our marriage. Operations ran smoothly as I managed responsibilities for our companies while he was in Thailand with his new girlfriend. We discussed separating on our own without involving lawyers. Then disagreements spurred heated confrontations which threatened my personal safety.

The emotional turmoil was a constant storm I couldn't escape. Layered on this was the division of our financial assets as we dealt with our bills and business expenses. Since my dream car was under the business name, it was taken away and I had no transportation. Disagreements about listings and ownership put the sale of our home in limbo. He canceled services with the cable, phone, and internet providers. He blocked me from our companies that I helped build. I was jobless and alone.

Joy was elusive as depression and anxiety weighed heavily on me. My health deteriorated. I could barely function. Antidepressants, anti-anxiety medications, and sleeping pills were prescribed for me. Later, I realized what I thought was rock bottom was truly a blessing.

Frederick Lorenz studied the short-term and decade-long effects of divorce on women's midlife health and found divorce has large effects on psychological distress as well as negative impacts on physical health (2006). Studying the effect of divorce on more than 400 women over a decade, he observed the process of getting a divorce is disruptive and can cause psychological distress — especially in the early stages. Over longer periods of time, the experience of being divorced leaves many women — like me — in disadvantaged social and economic situations which can impact physical health.

Left with nothing, I focused on myself and embraced self-care. I became curious about what made me happy. I read books, explored different types of music, and watched movies from all genres. I took long walks alone and experimented with various exercise classes. I surrounded myself with family and friends who lifted my spirits and reminded me of my strength.

Women suffer more financially from divorce than men do and the financial burden is greatest during the first year as assets and bills are negotiated. Uncertain about when my divorce would end and what the outcome would be, I faced many unknowns. I accepted that my financial reality in the present moment needed to change. I reached back to my previous career in finance in order to rebuild my financial security. I assessed my spending and determined the essentials. I paused discretionary spending for clothes, travel, and dining out at restaurants. I downsized my belongings and found a smaller place to live that suited my needs. When I developed my budget, I felt empowered knowing what I could (and could not) afford.

Working with a therapist put my life in perspective and opened the door to my emotional healing. I became accountable for my emotions and actions. As challenges arose, counseling allowed me to come to terms with my divorce and how my life was changing. Instead of wallowing in sadness or behaving irrationally, I felt empowered to act in my best interests.

Eight months into my separation, I attended a live, one-day event with Jack Canfield. The event changed me and my career trajectory. I connected with the community and the team. The experience ignited my spark. It was time to start taking control of my life in new and exciting ways. I discovered new opportunities going beyond managing my everyday needs. My future became brighter as I joined the community and participated in a mastermind group for additional support as well as Facebook groups. These groups opened my eyes to how many other people experienced similar challenges. I no longer felt alone and learned my struggles were part of a healing process.

Self-care was intertwined with my growth. Daily walks and drinking plenty of water became part of my routine. My readings increased and diversified as I embraced my curiosity. My inspiration grew as I listened to personal growth books like *The Success Principles* (Jack Canfield), *Daring Greatly* (Brene Brown) and *Abundance Now* (Lisa Nichols). I rebuilt and strengthened relationships with family and friends. Each day brought new learning about myself and opportunities like eCommerce, marketing, wellness, and coaching.

As another year passed, complications with the divorce grew more intense. Though I felt stronger emotionally, my health deteriorated. The drama of my divorce sidetracked my personal growth. My primary focus of self-care was sidelined. I gained 20 lbs., became borderline diabetic, and developed high cholesterol.

This was a pivotal moment. I could go on medications for life or take control of my health. I doubled down on myself and changed my eating habits and increased the intensity of my exercise. I wrote in my journal daily and practiced gratitude. My physical and emotional health improved. Within a few months, I felt stronger, happier and energized to keep moving forward.

I felt liberated and excited about my future as the divorce process dragged on. During each conflict that arose, I reflected on my progress. I discovered strategies for managing my stress including therapy and working with essential oils. I faced my finances directly and developed new ways of earning income through online sales on Amazon and Etsy. When selling to a niche market was not generating sufficient income, I pivoted and explored different items that could reach a broader audience. When challenges came, rather than isolating myself in shame and doubt, I connected with trusted friends and family to help me work through my problems. My relationships are stronger than before my marriage. I now surround myself with people who are authentic with positive energy and wanting more from life.

Pursuing self-care and happiness provided clarity for the next chapter in my professional journey. I discovered my purpose — helping others overcome the challenges of divorce. Building on my experience in finance and self-care, I possess the tools to help my clients transform their lives and achieve their goals. I help them redefine themselves, emerge stronger, and reclaim their power.

My divorce is not over but it does not define me nor does it control my happiness. My new life starts now instead of waiting for my divorce to end. I start each morning with a focus on what brings me joy — from listening to the birds in the morning on my walk to the images on the vision board beside my desk. The struggles that once isolated me now connect me with others. I am an entrepreneur, a coach, and consultant who helps clients explore their emotions, overcome shame, reclaim their power, and become better than before.

When we nurture the seed of hope within us, even during the throes of chaos and uncertainty, it can ignite growth, opportunities, and joy. 🏵

Kristin E. Sparks

❀

Kristin Sparks is a pull up your bootstraps kinda gal always landing on her feet no matter the life challenge. She is originally from Houston, Texas but has lived across this country from sea to shining sea. She is the mother of two daughters, one son, a daughter and a son in-law. One of her greatest Joys is being Grandma KK to her favorite seven grandchildren.

Kristin is a writer, speaker, Podcaster, philosopher, and the Executive Director of The Sister Wyrd Foundation, a Nonprofit supporting and celebrating women on their journey of self-transformation.

Kristin is genuinely grateful every day to enjoy the Floridian Salt Life in her chosen piece of paradise with her wife of many years, her pug, and her kitty. Kristin lives for and by Joy, allowing the true nature of the Divine Universe Source to direct and inspire her.

Contact
Website: https://flow.page/kristinsparks
Email: ks@kristinsparks.com

Dancing on the Wind of Life

By Kristin E. Sparks

"Joy is closer than you think"

— Marriot Bonvoy Ad

When I was asked to participate in this project, I hesitated and asked for time to consider it. While doing so, this quote, "Joy is closer than you think," came across my phone in an ad to get away to a beautiful destination. I knew it was a sign from the Universe to be in *The Book on Joy*.

The world is a crazy place right now. There is fear and anger in America and in my own backyard. It scares me. When I watch the news, talk to my neighbors and family, it's hard to get away from it entirely. Our normal routines have changed. Change is the nemesis for most people. There are industries dedicated to helping people deal with change, remain grounded, happy, and joyful. Trying to find meaning in our lives does not come easily when we are working to survive. We need to start small.

Choosing Joy is starting small. Joy is my "Thank you" first thing in the morning and my good night. Joy is my choice to be. Joy is all my love, failures, and successes. Joy feeds me and fills me. Joy overrides any negative sense, pushing it out by giving life to my pain, my lack, and bringing me back to gratitude. Joy resides in my cells. Joy works in and through me. Joy is my choice in life and my life in choice. Joy serves so that others may know the wonders of this world. Joy is the soul of life. Joy is the eyes, and the ears, of the Universal Source of Energy we are all a part of. Joy is perfect, sexy, and juicy. Joy fills a room and comes from the heart. Joy is a feeling, a sense of being. Joy can be found, it can be chosen, and it can be shared. It is always closer than we think.

Living is best in a state of Joy.

I use these three steps to find Joy in any moment . . .

1. Stop and breathe deeply for a count of 3.
2. Listen to nature-the birds chirping, the wind blowing, the water running, the voice of knowing.
3. Choose your attitude and live wildly.

I am Joy because I choose to be. At any time in my day, I choose my attitude, and when I choose joy, forgiveness, and gratitude, I am a happy, fun, and loving person. When I choose to be angry or mean, I get fired-up. I can cause pain to those I love or others around me, which only causes me to feel shame and guilt afterward.

So why do that when it only makes me and those around me miserable? My choice to take 100% responsibility for myself gives me a breath of fresh air, releases tension from my body, and allows me to be free. Free to love, free to appreciate the beauty and kindness around me, and it enables me to be free to choose JOY. I am a flawed and imperfect human. I still have many faults, but my outlook on life is positive even in the face of death, pain, suffering, abuse, and terror. I chose Joy because that is the gift we have been given, to live here in this life, this body, this mind, to these challenges, and to choose joy.

I grew up knowing I was a proud Texan even in the very fabric of my being. Knowing I was part of something bigger saved me from myself many times over the years. My motto inspired me to pull myself up by my bootstraps, Texas-style, when things got tough, that happened when I was young and even today. I am not sure when I first heard that motto, but it became ingrained in my psyche and gave my life a direction. Being a Texan is one of my joys.

Pregnancy and my ability to produce life changed me and my outlook. I loved the process of nine months, watching my body change in ways I was unaware it could. I had the power and honor of making and giving life. I was invincible and remarkable. Joy was my companion, as my body and heart became attached to these children in ways that allowed me to feel amazing. With all of its 'normal' and not so 'normal' challenges, motherhood brought me lessons I never would have known or appreciated without keeping Joy close. My children, and now my grandchildren, fuel my joy.

There was a light that began in my teenage years; granted, it only penetrated a tiny bit in my crazy, rage-filled mind and came in the form of my stepmother. I never allowed myself to get to know her directly, as I was a scared, little girl filled with pain, shame, and guilt. I was afraid she wouldn't love or like me, but I knew I wanted some of what she had. She was a petite Texas woman, a spitfire in her own right and strong and sweet. She was everything I wanted to be. I watched her take the rage out of my dad, and she was not going to stand for a man who took his fist and feet to the walls and doors. I watched her with her children, one a year younger than I and two out of the house; there was always laughter, respect, and love. I was amazed at her devotion to her faith, her family, and to us. I lost out on so many things with her as a young adult because I chose to wallow in my own mire, but I never quit admiring her from afar. She has taught me what it meant to be a Texas Woman, even if I didn't always heed that knowledge. Over the years, I have spent many a time trying to ignore her influence. Still, her light shined brighter in my soul than I could ever have known or appreciated until I was diagnosed with cancer last year. Her true grit and faith gave me such love and joy, as well as the fortitude to endure and thrive. My "mom" and the light she brings is my Joy.

My bestie and I have been together for over thirty-five years! It still amazes me that Sharon has put up with me for all this time. She was my salvation when I was getting divorced from my husband. She is my biggest champion and my best critic. Sharon is my confidant and my truth meter. She brings out the best and the worst in me. I could not have done, nor would I have wanted to miss out on, this life without her. She is the mother and the sister I wish I had growing up, and she is much more. I am lucky and grateful she is in this life with me. She brings out the adventurer in me and I in her.

In the fall of 1992, I had recently returned from Florida, where I survived Hurricane Andrew. I was feeling alive and needed an adventure weekend, and Sharon was on board to go. I did not tell her where we were going, I just picked her up on a Saturday afternoon and headed north to Lake Erie. Taking the last ferry of the day, we sailed out to the Island of Put-In-Bay. There we encountered the Tall Ship Exhibition. While partying in the 'Round Bar,' we met the crew from the tall ship known as 'The Provident.' The next day, the captain invited Sharon and I to join the crew in the reenactment of the battle of Lake Erie. I was hooked. They offered me the position of galley wench and asked that I join them in their continuing travels down to Tahiti. As I reached for my car keys, Sharon said, "You've got to be kidding me, not happening." The Universe provides, and when it does, all of life is a fun experience. Adventures and sailboats of any kind are my spectacular Joy, but Sharon is my pure Joy.

Many years later, I met the love of my life, not in the way I would have expected, but the Universe has a funny way of blowing our minds sometimes. My love, my soul mate in this life, came to me in the body of a woman. I tried for months to refuse this gift, but she continued to offer it, until one day when I told her someone else had asked me to marry him. She turned away from me, and the Universe said to me loud and clear, "If you let her go, you will be losing the best thing to ever happen to you. Stop her now and hold on tight." I have been holding on for the last 20 years and always will. Priscilla keeps me honest, grounded, and authentic. She is tough and soft, light and dark, positive and negative, and always genuine. My heart and soul belong to her and she to me. I am the luckiest woman in the world to have been given this gift of life with her in it. We have shared many challenges, both good and bad, and she has been my saving grace. I would not be here if not for her. She has been my champion when things were hard in my career and life. She took on the role of nurse and caretaker when I was injured and disabled, and enduring cancer treatments and recovering from surgery. She is my best friend and greatest love. She makes me laugh every day which gives me great joy. Priscilla is my extraordinary Joy.

I agreed to take on the many challenges of living this life, in this body. The challenges have taught me to embrace the Joy of asking for and receiving help. I am blessed to have many wonderful, amazing women, and a few fabulous men in my corner, precisely when I needed them. I have grown to know Joy from overcoming all the adversity, and I have discovered my dreams because of it. Life can still throw curveballs. I still have Imposter Syndrome at times. I go "There" every once in a while, and I can be intimidated in my head, by others for short bursts of time.

Joy is finding peace, and peace resides inside of me. Even when I am in pain, anger, or wallowing in my own insecurities or mess, I am still surrounded by those things that bring me Joy. I have a choice to choose Joy, and like dragonflies, I can let the negative go and dance on the wind of life. I choose Joy. It is always closer than I think. 🏵️

Angela I. Schutz

❋

A ngela I. Schutz is the Founder of Driven to Succeed Consulting, LLC — a career coaching company, helping hundreds land jobs, dispelling the myth that *there are no jobs out there!* She loves helping the unemployed go from hopelessness to employed! She also teaches HR Management, co-leads online clutter-clearing groups, and leads a woman's Dream Dare Dance group.

In 2012 she published her first book: *Career Questions? Ask Angela — A Job-seekers Guide to finding the Perfect Job.* Since 2012, she has co-authored 8 community books on gratitude and *A Woman's Journey — stories of Substance, Survival and Success.* In 2021 Angela wrote: *A Boomer Chick's Guide to Online Dating — You're Never Too Old to Look and Love.* Currently she is co-authoring *Clutter-Free at 73 — From Chaos to Clarity.*

She was inducted in Who's Who in America in 2020, and in Who's Who in Professional Women in 2021. Angela was humbled and honored by these awards. She resides in Connecticut.

Contact

Websites: www.driventosucceed.net and
www.boomer-chick.com

The Joy of Being a Big, Beautiful Woman

By Angela I. Schutz

"Carrying yourself with poise and joy and peace within — that's sexy."

— Leah LaBelle

I have lived the life of a plus-sized woman and have also experienced reducing 85 pounds so that I was considered a "normal-sized" woman, and I can tell you that there is a noticeable difference in the way plus-sized people are treated by society.

When I started thinking about what brings me joy, I knew I wanted to talk about the differences in the way a woman is treated based on her weight and offer some suggestions for overcoming the ridicule to get to a place of joy. These are tough issues, but I feel we need to look at them.

Let's start with the fashion world: Oh, we have heard the media deliver stories on the problems within the fashion world. Models have such a difficult time maintaining their skeleton-like figures. They literally starve themselves to keep their jobs. They work grueling schedules and consume so few calories that they can barely get through the day without fainting, and yet, to many women, these models represent the image of the "ideal woman."

On occasion we hear of "large" models trying to make a name in the industry. These so called "large" women are barely a size 12. It's considered a newsworthy event when a woman challenges the fashion world to look at the negative, psychological impact that is going on. It even filters down to very young girls who are concerned about their weight and feel they "need" to go on a diet.

Let's look at the psychological damage caused by being too focused on being thin. So many women struggle their entire lives trying to be thin and feeling like complete failures in life because they don't ever reach that goal. Often, the result is to begin a painful journey that includes eating disorders such as anorexia nervosa or bulimia. Statistically, 9% of the American society experience eating disorders at some time in their lives. These disorders are often shrouded in secrecy until the negative results become so apparent that medical treatment is the only hope for keeping the person alive.

Psychologists have a lot of patients who are troubled by the feelings of diminished self-worth. When they take a deep dive into the problem, they find that from an early age, these women felt the ridicule from being overweight.

Are you thinking, "What about the good health that results from being at your optimal weight?" Of course, you can always make the argument that one is far healthier when not carrying around too much weight. We have learned how damaging excess belly fat is and that too much cortisol damages your organs. Over time, high cortisol levels can lead to weight gain, high blood pressure, diabetes, fatigue and difficulty concentrating.

I would not refute the argument that it is healthier to be at your optimal weight, but do we, as a society, need to overpower people with both overt and subliminal messages to get the point across? Can't we find a more positive way to teach people to have a healthy lifestyle? Where is the compassion for others?

There are many reasons a person may be overweight. They may be experiencing psychological issues due to mental illness or trauma. They may be on medication that causes weight gain. They may have also experienced an injury that has immobilized them and reduced their normal activity. Whatever the reason, we need to stop making them feel like less of a person simply because they are not thin. Rather than making an instant, critical judgement of a person based on their weight, wouldn't it be better to realize that you don't know what the person has been through and being critical of their weight may cause you to overlook all of the amazing skills and talents they have?

We are painfully aware of the discrimination that is aimed at minority groups. There is also a tremendous amount of discrimination against the aged and the obese. We get a glimpse of the problem when we hear about children hurting themselves because they were bullied due to their weight. It is so painful to hear of a child taking their own life because they were ostracized for being overweight.

Many women feel that same discrimination of their weight but say nothing. They feel the abusive slurs every time a comment is made about their weight. We shrug it off when a woman asks: "Do these pants make me look fat?", but isn't she really exhibiting a cry to fit in?

There may be some everyday negative situations that happen in the lives of those who are overweight that may not occur to people who have never had a weight problem. For example, unless you have been excessively overweight, you cannot possibly know how embarrassing it is to sit down in the seat of an airplane, only to find out that the seat belt doesn't fit, and perhaps even to be asked to leave the plane for lack of compliance with the law.

I worked in the Admitting Department of a hospital for many years. When an obese patient needed to be admitted, we were instructed to call for the "Big Bertha" wheelchair to transport them to their room. It is so hard to have this ill person sitting across from you nervously waiting to be admitted into the hospital and you must make a call asking for the "Big Bertha"! Is that not insensitive behavior?

How do all those amazing, overweight people find love? Well, they can go to dating sites like Big Beautiful People Meet! There, they can really call attention to the fact that no one will choose them or love them on the "regular" dating sites! Attention to their excess weight is immediately showcased. The saddest part is that they are often so starved for positive attention they become the targets for the scammers who convince them that if they give them money, the man will use it to put a down payment on a house where they will live "happily ever after" as a couple.

These men profess undying love for this woman who may have never experienced love before. She believes him. She so wants to be loved and to feel like a real woman. She will give him enormous amounts of money to feel they are truly "partners". I have heard of women giving up to one million dollars to men they have never even met in person! She has no idea her emotions are being played with. She may have been shunned so often that she possesses little to no self-worth.

As a parent and grandparent, myself, it truly bothers me when I see so many children, overweight or not, being ignored. In their formative years, children need to experience the joy of having a strong sense of self-worth. They weren't born with it, so it is up to the adults in their lives to help instill it in them. One powerful way to do this is by validating the things they do right and by gently encouraging them to learn and grow.

What can you do if you are a big, beautiful woman and your family is the "discouragement committee"? Do they constantly remind you that you would look better or have a boyfriend if you would just take off some weight? Don't fall prey to all that negativity. I promise you that every time you move toward having a positive attitude about who you really are, you should celebrate it as a victory. You are not your weight, nor does excess weight diminish the skills and talents you have. Take some time to recognize your talents because they belong to you, and you alone. They are a gift. You did nothing to have those talents, but you can work to develop them.

One thing I have learned is that what we put our mind on grows. Picture yourself as a vibrant, happy, joyous woman who knows who she is and truly loves the woman she has become. Picture yourself as the person everyone wants to spend time with because you radiate joy. You are the first one to be invited to a party. You love your curves and know that those flowing clothes are the perfect covering for your vibrant, curvaceous body. Feel how great it feels to be loved and desired as a woman. Know that our bodies are like a suit of clothing we wear, but in reality, it is our mind and spirit that are really the keys to living a joyous life, no matter what our body looks like.

There is an expression that works here: "fake it 'til you make it."

Picture yourself joyous until you are filled with joy. Picture yourself radiating beauty. Know that anything you can imagine can come true. When you see someone staring at you, imagine they are thinking: "Look at that beautiful woman!" and flash them a big smile!

There is nothing more joyous than that feeling of self-confidence that comes from knowing and appreciating your talents. People who care about themselves tend to care more about others. Self-confidence is a joyous thing. It makes you walk taller, smile more, have a glint in your eye and feel sexy. You feel invincible because you know there is always someone who has your back . . . it's you!

On that magical day, when you move out of the state of low self-worth and into the state of self-confidence you will experience pure joy. You will also experience the joy of knowing you can handle the things that come your way. Embrace the joy that is completely from the inside and the joy in feeling that sense of, "I got this".

If you are a big, beautiful woman, step into your own beautiful skin and know that you, too, deserve the joy that comes from owning who you are and how much this world needs you right now! Joy is your birthright. There is nothing more beautiful and sexier than a woman who knows and appreciates who she is. Celebrate your uniqueness, develop your natural talents, and most of all, love the woman you are. 🏵

Victoria Chadderton

---❈---

Victoria Chadderton is an author, trainer, speaker and Distinguished Toastmaster. She works with transformational leaders training, facilitating workshops and retreats. She is an Amazon Best Selling author. Her work with the Law of Attraction has brought out her passion for helping others visualize and obtain what brings them JOY!

In addition, she has been active in local community organizations, such as Boy Scouts of America, Washington Elementary PTSA and Women's Service League. Currently she is the District Director of District 9 Toastmasters. Victoria lives in Washington State and enjoys spending time with her family, going on family vacations and exploring new places.

Contact

Website: www.victoriachadderton.com
Email: chadderton.victoria@gmail.com

Journey Back to Joy

By Victoria Chadderton

"The deeper that sorrow carves into your being,
the more joy you can contain."

— Kahlil Gibran

What brings you JOY? That question was posed to me at a time when I thought I would never experience joy again. Loss and grief can do that to a person. If I were to ask you that question, would you have an instant answer, or would you have to think about it? How long would it take you to come up with that answer? When it was asked of me, I was numb. I didn't want to feel anything.

Growing up, I experienced feelings and emotions to my core. When I was happy, I was beaming. People would comment that I had a glow about me when I was in the moment of enjoyment. However, the Universe seems to have an opposite force, perhaps to keep balance. When I was sad, I felt sadness to my core. I would feel the dark heaviness upon me and those around me could feel it too. I would stay in this state like a black cloud hovering over me.

As I grew older, I wanted to spend less time feeling sad, so I learned to release those feelings. I realized that my ability to fully experience positive emotions was a gift, because when I have such an intense connection to these feelings, my days are more enjoyable; I can navigate the world easier.

For example, when something does not go the way you thought it would, how do you react? When you are in a negative state of mind, it can feel like the world is falling apart. When you are in a positive state of mind, you are able to course correct faster and get back on track to achieving your goals.

I was in my 40's when I met a fun, wonderful man who loved me.

We had only been married for six months when he was diagnosed with renal failure. In the beginning, I looked at this challenge as simply a bump in our journey. I must admit that my friends thought that I had turned into Pollyanna. We were in love and I chose to see the situation in a positive light, believing we could get through this together. Luckily, I had a job that allowed me to go to all his doctors' appointments and be there to support and encourage him. At first, I was researching and asking the doctors many questions. Making sure I was there during hospital procedures to ensure that the level of care was being met, made feel good . . . like I was taking care of things. As time went on, we got into a routine. However, over the next two years his health continued to decline. I got angry! Angry at him, the doctors, the Universe and myself. The dark clouds started to collect once again. Just as in my youth, the anger was unproductive and created tension.

My husband and I discussed what health directives he wanted in place. I knew intellectually what he wanted, but my heart was torn. I did not want my love to suffer or be in pain, but I did not want to say goodbye to the hugs and "I love you's" either.

After he had been in the hospital for over a month, the time came when I knew I needed to be his advocate once more and make the tough medical decisions. Fortunately, I had gone through hospice before and knew the basics of how it would all play out. I had to sign the paperwork to stop all life-support and allow nature to take its course. His family and I were with him. We had time to say, "I love you" and "goodbye".

After his passing, I tried to keep myself busy . . . distracting myself from going through the grief process. I was not ready to feel all the pain, so . . . I went to workshops. That is where I was asked, "What brings you JOY?" I could think of things that had brought me joy in the past, but how could I possibly feel joy now that my love was gone. I chalked up my response to being 'too soon'. In reality, I hadn't taken time to grieve.

I don't remember how long it had been when I was driving in the car one day, listening to the radio. I always had it on for background noise. That first note started and I immediately knew which song it was: Low Rider by War. It was his song! My heart skipped a few beats but I kept listening. I found myself smiling for the first time since his passing. Music had been one of the areas that we really connected with each other. He would play a song and then we would talk about what memories it brought up for one another. It was our way of connecting and learning more about each other. Having met later in life and each having a past with others, we did not have that gift of time before.

Not only did we connect over music but dance as well. He was such a trooper. When we first started dating, Zumba fitness was becoming a worldwide exercise sensation. He encouraged me to take the class to become a certified Zumba instructor. But most of all he would go with me to Zumba classes. We didn't care how we looked we were having fun and enJOYing our time with each other. I don't do as many classes now, but I still find joy when I go to a class. I have learned to allow the feelings to flow through me and dance helps with that a lot. There are times when a certain song will come on that will bring back wonderful memories and I can now remember the joy that I felt. I hope you have memories that bring you joy as well.

Remember the question, "What brings you JOY?" I actually made a list of things that have brought me joy in the past and things that I can do today that bring me joy. I encourage you to do the same. They can be big things, like the joy of holding my grandson for the first time. They can be precious moments such as the joy in giving a friend a bouquet of flowers. They can be small things such as dancing to a song that comes on the radio in your living room.

I've learned this truth: Life is too short to hold onto the dark clouds. I am grateful for all that I have learned through the dark moments, and I hope the same for you. When I feel the clouds rolling in, I look at my list of what I might do to bring joy into the world, and then go out and do it. 🏵️

Paddy Briggs

❀

Paddy was raised in a small retail business. She married and had three daughters. Some time ago, Paddy found herself on her own with her three girls. She realized she had to develop a career. Without post-secondary education she transitioned what skills she had to working on the front desk of a dental office. This was the start of her journey. She expanded from there to managing dental practices, teaching a Dental Receptionist Program, and then Practice Management Consultant & Trainer specializing in dentistry. Her approach has always been one of collaboration and thoughtful coaching and training.

In 2019 she graduated as a Jack Canfield — Certified Transformational Coach. Paddy is using this opportunity to enhance her passion to work with women who are either in transition in their career / business or their personal life. This new division within her company will be working with women who want to take charge of their life, empowering them to "live their best life."

Contact
Website: www.paddybriggs.ca

Finding Joy
Through Perseverance

By Paddy Briggs

"Let your joy be in your journey —
not in some distant goal."

— Tim Cook

The reason why this quote speaks to me is because it took me a long time to realize I needed to tap into, spend time and be grateful for the joy I felt as my journey took me closer and closer to my goal. I was so focused on reaching my goal that I did not see nor feel the joy in achieving one step at a time.

I was 39 years old, married with three daughters in the middle of a devastating global recession.

We lost everything! I found myself in a serious financial state. My husband went to another province to find work and I discovered he was living with a 26-year-old. I suddenly found myself alone with my three daughters to support. I was devastated and terribly afraid. 'How on earth was I going to do this? What was I going to do?' No education, no degree. My background prior to marrying was a small family retail business, and secretarial work. That would not support the four of us. 'What joy is there in this situation? This is devastating. I can't do this. I can't support myself and three kids!'

Everyone has a story. I imagine you do too. I have heard it said that our stories define us. I do not know about that. I think our stories and our life experiences are very important. They help develop us and create who we are.

This is my story!

I had a fear of not having enough and not being enough, these were my limiting beliefs that I had to overcome. I was not sure what to do — what did I need? I needed to change my mindset, my belief of not having enough was limiting me. I needed to stop thinking I'm not enough, I can't do this, I'm not smart enough, I'm not educated enough.

I knew I must find a job. I had $900.00 in the bank and $500.00 of it would go to rent. I got a job through a friend photocopying all day long. The employer was a Pulp & Paper Consultant who travelled all over the world training people in the industry. My responsibility was to make sure his very large training manuals included every single page, perfectly copied, so not only did I photocopy, then I had to go through each page to ensure every single page was there. The job didn't pay enough to support the four of us, so I took a job on weekends and 2 nights a week in retail, Women's Clothing.

As I stood for 8 hours every day I began to think, is this it — is this all? During this time, I was given a set of Jack Canfield — Self Esteem and Peak Performance tapes. As I began to listen to them, something rose up inside of me. I began to realize I could do this — I was destined for more. I had some transferable skills. I very slowly started to believe in myself.

I started to do some research as to what I wanted to do. I knew I wanted to be in a service profession. I had a passion for helping people. I also knew I had to make a decent income so I would not have to work seven days a week. I finally decided on administrative, working on the front desk of a dental office. I took a night school course, two nights a week for three months which taught me the basics. It was enough training to get my first job in dentistry. Yay — I was off!

I worked on the front desk for approximately five years learning all I could. I was very fortunate to have an office manager who saw something in me that I obviously did not see! She asked me what my goals were? Where did I want to go in dentistry? I told her I wanted to manage a dental office. She insisted I take the weekend and develop a personal Vision for myself, set my goals as to what I wanted and how I was going to get there. What an amazing exercise for me.

Not too long after that a Practice Management Consultant offered me a management position, managing two practices. She also saw something in me that I didn't see! She then asked me to take over teaching a part time Dental Receptionist Program. She had developed the curriculum and taught this for a few years and didn't want to teach anymore. My response was "Oh sure — I'll do that for you!" It was shortly after I was asked to develop and teach a part time Dental Office Receptionist Program at one of the colleges in the Fraser Valley. A two-week practicum in a dental office was a component of the program. I would monitor each student, which I loved. It was through monitoring that I began to get calls from dentists or their managers asking me to help them with various issues they were facing in their business. That is how my career began as a Practice Management Consultant & Trainer, specializing in dentistry.

Wow, who would ever have thought that I could achieve this! I didn't think I had the courage, the knowledge nor the strength to do what I needed to do but I DID! I am so grateful for my divorce — if it wasn't for my husband leaving us, I would not be where I am today.

Step out, believe in yourself; remember there is nothing you cannot achieve; you have everything you need to achieve your goals. Be open and welcome change because it's change that creates growth. Above all, don't get so caught up in achieving the goal that you miss the experience of joy in each step, always look for the joy in your journey and celebrate your successes.

If I can do this you can too!

Choosing

JOY

❁ ❁ ❁ ❁ ❁

Robin Eldridge Hain

❀

Robin Hain had a thirty-year career with Colgate-Palmolive Company, managing $10 Million annualized retail Sales. She is a seven-time recipient of the internal company award for excellence and one external trade partner vendor of the year award.

Robin graduated with a Bachelor of Science in Psychology, which has served as a strong foundation for her continued pursuit of best practices in Mental Health, Substance Use Disorder and Trauma Restoration.

Her mission is to end stigma and advocate for policy changes that support long-term recovery systems of care.

Her volunteer service includes board member for www.MWVsupportsrecovery.org and www.sicd-fl.org. Robin is also a Shatterproof Ambassador (Shatterproof.org) and developing a Recovery Strong Community.org web-based platform.

She and her husband, Scott, reside in Sarasota, Florida and Silver Lake, New Hampshire. They enjoy traveling the world and cherish time spent with family and friends.

Contact
Email: Robin_Hain@yahoo.com

Fearlessly Choosing Joy

By Robin Eldridge Hain

*"Joy is a decision, a really brave one,
about how we are going to respond to life."*

— Wess Stafford

Joy resides in my heart and soul. It is either active or resting. When present, it resonates with a supernatural power to heal whatever ails me and propels me to new heights. My spirit is lifted to the sky on wide-spread wings and set down like a feather in awe.

Joy inspires growth and makes everything seem possible.

Joy was Mooney, my very first best friend. She had red, curly hair that brushed her shoulders and a smile from ear-to-ear. She filled my days with joy. That was until my Auntie Val sat on the sofa right on top of her. I immediately yanked Mooney free, "You are sitting on Mooney!" I exclaimed. I fearlessly defended Mooney, as that is what friends do. My mother's raised arm pointed toward my bedroom, where I was banished to play quietly until Auntie Val left. I was the only one who saw Mooney. Eventually, she moved away and just the thought of her makes me smile.

I struggled in my neighborhood elementary school that had three rooms with five grades. My brother mastered all his lessons with ease. I decided not to participate in spelling bees that widened the gap between the best and worst students. I did know many of the words as one-by-one classmates took their seats until the spelling wizard took the trophy one more time. You know, it isn't always the last kid standing who is the smartest.

Finally, in fourth grade, I found a subject I excelled in. It was short division. I aced my first quiz. I knew I did. The teacher always handed back our test results from best to worst. Why was I the last one to get mine? How could I know she changed her method that day? Seeing the red "A" at the top of the quiz I turned, toward my classmates, "I got an A!" They appeared stunned by my outburst. I didn't wait for the dismissal bell. I immediately ran out the schoolhouse door and skipped all the way home to put my first "A" on the refrigerator door.

It was in moments like these that I continued to make joy my priority in life.

In my junior year I blossomed into many leadership roles just in time to realize I wanted to go to college; a goal that my early educators never saw coming. I then learned my family had not set aside the funds for college. This was a shock given that we were doing lots of fun things as a family throughout my childhood. We were either on the water sailing out of Newport, Rhode Island, or hiking and skiing in Mt. Washington Valley, New Hampshire (NH). My father was a self-employed designer and builder of homes and boats. He always cleared his schedule when school was out. Work-life balance was my father's priority, which set the foundation for terrific family memories. Even at a young age I knew this was something special. There seemed to be no limit to life's adventures when you were willing to work hard. Many nights when my homework was finished, I would go to my Dad's workshop to help him sweep up at the end of a long day.

It was now up to me to take charge of my future starting with getting into the best, most affordable four-year college I could find.

I did it! After graduating with a Bachelor of Science in Psychology and School Guidance, I was hired as an Elementary School Guidance Counselor under a NH State Grant. I traveled between five elementary schools in rural Mt. Washington Valley. I developed a curriculum based on the *Warm Fuzzy Tale* book by Claude Steiner. Through art therapy, role playing, breathing and stretching exercises, the program was designed to reduce stress and build self-esteem in the at-risk students I served. Further, I invited the students' families to contact me with any questions about this new program. I received no questions or calls. Basic needs of food and clothing were provided by school and community programs. However, the relationships I made with some of these students lasted long past the one-year grant period. One student taught me to ride horseback which she got quite a chuckle out of. The students taught me that we all come with joy and the ability to access it regardless of the circumstances.

A friend encouraged me to visit her in Alexandria, Virginia (VA). She was looking for a roommate, and I was looking for a change. I spent all of my free time exploring Washington D.C. and the Smithsonian Museums. The power of our democracy and the cost to preserve it filled the air. The cherry trees were in full bloom surrounding the city when I applied for a job with the Colgate-Palmolive Company. I was hired in a three-month, three-man race for one job. Before I knew it, I was the last "man" standing. There were only a handful of women in sales at that time, and most of my co-workers were like brothers lifting me up. I received invaluable mentoring which allowed me to achieve year-over-year growth in my various positions that I held with the company for 30 years.

The Philadelphia Marketplace offered me a promotion and the opportunity to jumpstart my life as I was dissolving my marriage of less than a year. I married because I was 28 because I forgot to get married and raise a family. Our incompatibility became clear within months of the union. A clue that it was time to move on came to light when I returned home from work with food for the freezer, only to find it was filled with marijuana. Seriously, who needs that much pot? The final straw was when I discovered he gambled away $100,000 at the track. He was clearly not interested in sharing anything with me, including freezer space. I moved in with my aunt, godmother and friend, Sue and her family in St. Davids, Pennsylvania (PA), while I looked for my own place. Her friendship framed my faith that my hopes and dreams would still come true. My new townhouse was filled with sunshine as old friends visited and new friendships developed. This space provided me with clarity about the type of man with whom I wanted to build a life — a life of joy and adventure.

I found him! The Universe provided as Scott and I started our life together. We have been married for thirty-three years. It seems like a flash in time as we traveled this journey united in achieving our individual and joint goals. We knew we only had so much time before Scott's children Mike (13) and Maggie (10) were grown. The home we choose and the vacations we planned kept them front and center. Their childhood laughter still echoes in my heart. I have been so blessed to witness their life paths emerge.

Our desire to expand our family following seven unsuccessful rounds of IVF treatments led us to consider our local child welfare programs. Attending the foster-adoption certification program it became clear there was a match for everyone through this system. When the call came, we were told there was a one-year-old little boy living with his grandparents who were seeking a forever family for their grandson. We knew when we met them that they would be an essential part of his life. His birth mother could have been my sister, long brown hair just like I had at the age of sixteen. Nevin came to live with us when he was 18 months old. He immediately settled in sleeping through the night and engaging in all aspects of his new home life. Our open adoption was finalized before Nevin's second birthday, and our family doubled in size to include his birth family whose love and support throughout the years added to my joy.

Through the years Nevin expanded our appreciation of sports. He embraced athletics to the point we thought he was channeling Howard Cosell. At twelve Nevin was a homerun hitter. He received so many game balls he asked the coach if he would consider giving the game ball to the most improved player. His sportsmanship was appreciated by all who attended his games. We enjoyed many years traveling on cruises ships, visiting our national parks, Costa Rica, skiing in NH and vacationing in the Outer Banks.

Our family has again doubled in size with grandchildren and their extended families. The unique personality of each grandchild has enough fearless energy and joy to fill the universe. They give me hope for the future of humanity.

Girlfriends, soul sisters, we fearlessly supported each other through the years. Our bond was our armor. We biked and hiked. We built tree houses and real houses. We explored the rivers and lakes in various boats. We supported each other through breakups and makeups. We celebrated surprise birthday parties, weddings, big and small, our children, careers, and favorite vacation spots throughout the years. Oh, so much joy and laughter, my soul sisters, you are the glue, my chosen family. I celebrate our bond with deep gratitude as I look back on how far we have come.

Hiking to the summit of Mt Washington and Mt Chocorua since I was 12 has been an empowering annual highlight. Cresting these summits fueled my soul with the belief that anything in the coming year was possible. I discovered the impact of fear on a mountainside trail, in early spring, at the age of forty. I froze approaching a large section of blue-ice. The thought of not making it to the submit crossed my mind as fear of falling weakened my knees. Suddenly, two younger women sped ahead over the blue ice not missing a beat, one turned back to me and said, "Give me your arm!" Locked together by the elbows, one-two-three steps later and the ice was behind me. In that leap, I realized the impact of fear on joy. In that leap, I fearlessly chose joy. Each of the challenges to follow proved that *"Joy is a decision, a really brave one, about how we are going to respond to life."*

I awoke in the middle of the night to my husband's grand mal seizure. The local hospital MRI identified a brain tumor. I reached out to my Aunt Sue, who connected us to the Head of Neurosurgery at the University of Pennsylvania. The neurosurgeon removed the walnut-size oligodendroglioma. Six months of chemotherapy and radiation followed. The unwavering confidence in the medical care, support of family and friends, fueled my fearless support of Scott in his recovery.

My mother had fought a 6-year battle, with breast cancer as one chemo stopped working and another took its place until the side effects out-weighted the benefits. I decided if ever I was confronted with this disease, I would opt for a bi-lateral mastectomy. Thanks to the improved imaging, my biannual mammogram showed stage one lobal and ductal carcinoma. Off with the old and on with the new, I survived breast cancer without chemo and radiation. Some say every time we make a plan God laughs. I think God helps those who help themselves. They say you never know what you will do until directly confronted with the challenge. Fearlessly anticipating the plan saved precious time. To live in a time with many options opened space for joy and celebrations.

Nevin was in high school when the disease of addiction hijacked his brain. The disease of addiction challenges the strongest of families. During this ten-year journey our family has cycled through remission, recovery and relapse. Through continuous self-education I have channeled my energies in family support groups, local boards and advocacy work. The isolation of the Covid-19 pandemic has resulted in 1 in 4 American's suffering from mental health and substance use disorder. The millions of people in long term recovery give us strength and hope for those suffering with the disease of addiction.

Every day we celebrate the joys we share.

Facing any life-threatening condition, fear can bring us to our knees. Fearlessly seeking solutions to life's challenges, have led to joy in the most unexpected ways. The whisper in the wind or the chirping of the birds. Joy is the sunshine on a cloudy day. Joy is the gentle breeze that dries up all the rain. Joy can enter our life as a whisper or as the roar of a stadium filled with cheering fans. Joy massages all challenges, releasing the power of the universal symphony, healing the troubles of the world.

Fearlessly receive the outreached hand, the wisdom of those who have gone before you, the strength of community.

Pause to make room for the healing power of joy. 🏵

Notes

Andreava Kasianchuk

────❀────

Andreava's brilliance is rooted in breaking down complex ideas and rebuilding with purpose. With a Bachelor of Science in Strategic Communication and a background in Project Management, she has taken her education and previous experience in the Vacation Rental Industry to pivot onto an entrepreneurial path. As the founder of Create and Fulfill Consulting, Andreava finds joy in collaborating with small business owners and non-profit organizations who are passionate about what they do, to get clear on their goals, identify obstacles, and offer solutions and ongoing guidance to effectively stay on track. With an eye for visual design and the user's experience, her expertise extends to website development as well.

When she isn't taking a deep dive into others' passion projects, Andreava can be found outdoors on her skis or bike, where she feels most alive. From the White Mountains to the Colorado Rockies and back, Andreava currently resides in New Hampshire's Mount Washington Valley, where the journey to joy all began.

Contact
Website: www.createandfulfillconsulting.com

Trusting Joy

By Andreava Kasianchuk

"May you continue to open yourself up to the experience of joy, being okay with not knowing what awaits on the other side of it."

— Morgan Harper Nichols

At one time I was living what I would consider my dream life, residing in a small ski town nestled up against Colorado's rugged Rocky Mountains. Before heading into work most days, I'd clip into my skis to scale the local ski area and enjoy the free-floating sensation of fresh powder turns on the way down. It was often the stillness of those mornings before many were awake when I felt most alive—the sun just beginning to creep over the peaks, the chairlift chairs suspended in time, the brisk cool air kissing my cheeks, the thumping of my heart in my chest, and the view of the Continental Divide, so close, giving the illusion I could put my hand out and touch it.

It was the feeling that *I've arrived. I'm here now. I'm living this moment.*

I had ventured out to Colorado shortly after college with the intention of working a seasonal gig, yet what was to be six months eventually turned into eight years. My role and passion for teaching cross-country skiing led to a position in the vacation rental industry where I had the opportunity to continue to share my love for the area. This afforded me the lifestyle I wanted to live: endless powder days, gorgeous sunsets, mountain biking through wildflowers, paddling down thrilling rapids, sharing my backyard with many a moose, and inhaling fresh mountain air daily. I belonged to a community that warmed my heart and gave me the sense that *I'm home.*

What more could a gal ask for?

Thinking back, there were so many moments where I thought my heart would explode for the experiences my life continued to offer while residing in Colorado. This sentiment was echoed by many in the area, as it was not uncommon to hear someone ask, "How's it going?" and get the response "Doing, great! Living the dream." Being in this place embodied so much of what I was looking for in life, and while I continued to appreciate this dream, little did I realize at the time how tightly I was holding onto it.

In 2018, my body began to give me little nudges, reminders that I was in need of a change. This came in the form of neck tension and persistent headaches, lingering symptoms from a previous concussion, which were exacerbated by daily computer use. Not willing to accept that my job might be causing harm, especially with a belief that my work provided me the life I wanted to live, I sought out medical help to curb the symptoms. While I saw some improvements in this area of my health, for unknown and unrelated reasons, I began experiencing pelvic pain. Reluctant to see the bigger picture and a strong desire to hold onto the good, I began another search for answers. This led to more appointments with more specialists.

Looking back, I was scared to let go. I clung to my job, the foundation for all things I desired, not to mention the provider of health benefits to support my path to pain relief. I believed that if I were to leave this, I'd be letting go of all the good as well; that life couldn't get any better and this was its best.

And yet the very mountains that brought me joy began to feel distant and the little nudges I was experiencing started to come in the form of messages: I can't do this anymore. This isn't me. This can't be all that there is to life. There has to be something more...something else. It was the acknowledgement of my truth that allowed me to realize I can have gratitude for the joys of my past, while knowing that I am worthy of more — WE ALL ARE — and trusting that in the letting go, more joy will flow.

At the time, my closest friends, family, and health practitioners could see that I was in need of a change. Yet, I'm grateful they allowed me to come to this conclusion on my own and in the process, supported me every step of the way. Along this path of rediscovering and returning to joy there were some key events and insights that helped, which I'd like to share in hopes they may help you too:

1. Step Away (whatever that may look like for you)

In June of 2019, a close friend invited me to join her for a long weekend filled with camping, swimming in hot springs, and attending a day of the Telluride Bluegrass Festival. While my work world was busier than ever and I didn't know how I'd swing the time off, in my heart I knew I needed to be there.

As we left town to weave across the scenic state of Colorado, the flood gates opened and endless tears began to fall from my eyes. I was so confused. How could I be crying when I was simultaneously departing on a mini-vacation and surrounded by so much beauty? As the miles between myself and my everyday life increased, I began to sense how I was truly feeling.

That weekend's activities fed my soul, incorporating a combination of my staple joys — live music, travel, and time with friends — but ultimately it was the act of physically leaving town that allowed me to gain perspective and admit to myself that I wanted something different for my life. This continued to ring true as we drove home, the knots in my stomach tightened as we drew closer, and the thought of staying put grew more uncomfortable than the thought of change.

It wasn't long after that trip, I received a call 'out of the blue' from a close friend and mentor about a potential job opportunity, an initial seed to recultivate joy in my life.

A weekend trip isn't always an option, but finding a way to separate yourself from your everyday spaces, even for 24 hours, can help to differentiate emotions and offer clarity.

2. Accomplishments Aren't Everything

Up until this point I was a "go-getter," living for the achievements, checking things off the list, getting tasks done, and often feeling satisfaction and empowerment in doing so. Yet when my physical pain emerged and I continued on this engrained pathway, I was left feeling more and more exhausted. Without realizing it, much of my worth and identity had become tied up in my accomplishments. While I appreciated my ability to complete tasks, I kept getting the message that who I was, wasn't about what I did, and that I didn't need to withhold joy until I got something done. Additionally, continuing to operate in this way (from an empty cup) wasn't sustainable, nor would it positively serve me or others.

As directed by a coach, little by little I looked to add at least 1% more joy into my day, which required remembering what brought me joy. Once I had a go-to list of joys, my 1% sometimes looked like asking myself, "What would make this more fun?" In some cases, this was walking to the local coffee shop to order myself a specialty coffee drink before diving into a daunting work task. Sometimes it was sitting outside in the fresh air and sun for ten minutes or calling a friend. Over time, I embraced unplanned joy, marking time in my calendar to do "nothing," in turn creating a space for joy to seep in. Sometimes this literally looked like doing nothing, or sometimes it was saying "yes" to an impromptu invite.

I'll be honest, in this process, I realized I had been off the path of joy for quite some time. It felt difficult to choose *me*. As I consistently added 1% more joy to my life, my cup began to fill. I started to feel more like myself, remembering what was important to me and making the most of what soon became my remaining time in Colorado.

3. Options, Time, and What You Love Will Follow

It's funny how when you finally admit to yourself you want change, both the unknown of what's to come and the safety of what is, test this desire.

As someone who considered herself a "planner," during this time, I'd wavered between excitement and fear. I often felt overwhelmed with what a new and different life could look like. During this time of uncertainty, my health specialist provided a sense of ease by reminding me:

- I have options
- I don't have to figure it all out tonight
- If I know what I love, I can recreate it

Whenever I was stressed, I reminded myself of this, which gave me hope when I confronted a roadblock. It allowed me to say "yes" more often to spending time with a friend or doing something that brought me joy, even if my to-do list said otherwise (there will always be more to do). This also allowed me to trust that in choosing a new path and knowing both myself and my desires, my favorite joys, and even new joys, would follow.

It was from here that I continued to take small action steps each day and started to feel the momentum and see the possibilities of something better for my life.

Flash forward to now...

I currently reside in New Hampshire's Mount Washington Valley. While I never thought I'd return to my roots, I made the cross-country trek to embark on an entrepreneurial career path which feels in true alignment with my heart. I'm happy to report that in listening to what felt right for me, I'm pain-free. As I was told, some of my cherished joys followed me, such as having great access to skiing and mountain biking. In trusting this process, new joys have flowed like growing my own veggie garden and sharing spontaneous moments with my family.

I'm not advocating for anyone to leave a job, town, or abandon any aspect of their life, but instead to lean into choosing joy more often. This is the key to being able to clearly listen to your heart, remembering you're worthy of more joy and that it always awaits. Joy isn't necessarily a place, but a feeling that can be felt anywhere and at any time.

Joy is also a journey. Hold onto it loosely, knowing, like life, it's ever-flowing and changing. You may not be able to see it, but trusting that it's there, it can show up, and perhaps in better ways than you could imagine. 🏵

Sakshi Salve

Sakshi was born and raised in New Delhi, India. She received her bachelor's degree in Business Management in 2004 from the University of Exeter in the UK.

Sakshi is the best-selling author of, *The Big Indian Wedding*, published in September 2015. She also studied food science and tastings at the renowned Le Cordon Bleu Culinary School in London.

In 2020, as the world started preparing for a 'reset' due to Covid-19, Sakshi discovered that she could help people shift from a mindset of '*surviving*' to one of '*thriving*'. Having been through difficult times herself, she has a strong sense of compassion for others and naturally gravitated towards Life Coaching.

Sakshi is a certified Canfield trainer, is qualified to teach the Success Principles, has her PCC (Professional Coach Certification) from the reputed Rayner Institute in Canada and is also a certified 'Professional Executive Coach'. She is currently pursuing advanced PQ (Positive Intelligence) training (Under Shirzad Chamine).

Contact
Website: www.sakshisalve.com
Instagram: @sakshisalve

Unlocking the Cage

By Sakshi Salve

"Joy comes to us in the ordinary moments. We risk missing out when we get too busy chasing down the extraordinary."

— Brene Brown

I yearned to find my calling in life. I prayed for my life purpose to be revealed. I wanted to be good at something; wanted to make a difference. I wanted to jump out of bed every morning with child-like enthusiasm. I wanted to laugh again, wanted to feel loved and cherished again, I wanted joy back in my life again. But I was stuck. My beliefs kept me trapped, in a cage of my own making.

My story begins in 1983, the year I was born, in the metropolitan city of New Delhi, India. I grew up in a beautiful home with my parents and a younger sister. I had a secure and privileged childhood that shielded me from many difficulties and blessed me with experiences that created immense joy growing up.

I was fascinated with everything adult, and I couldn't wait to grow up and be one myself. When I was five, I loved to wrap myself in my mother's elegant chiffon sarees, put on her darkest red lipstick and walk around the bedroom pretending like I was all grown up. By the time I was ten, I was 'teaching' imaginary students in my bedroom, on my little black board, a gift from my mother. Whenever my cousins came over to play, our favorite game was ghar-ghar, which literally translated means house-house. We all pretended to be adults and would assume the roles of our parents and other relatives. Life was simple and blissful.

Moving on to my teenage years, I have some lovely memories of sitting in the back seat of a rented car, earphones in my ears, Discman on my lap, and blaring music going right into my brain. We took a month-long family vacation every summer. My father driving us around Europe, Scotland or the US, my mother singing old Bollywood songs, my sister peacefully drooling in her sleep, and me, enjoying the moving scenery and my music. There is something cathartic about long drives. I could sit for 12 hours just looking out the window, listening to music and allowing my imagination to peek out of the box. The long periods of inner silence let me tap into the tiny spaces between my thoughts. These were precious fleeting moments of absolute 'nothing-ness', my mind completely blank like a fresh new canvas ready to be painted on.

Growing up, I didn't know much about this rollercoaster we call life. From the highest highs to the lowest lows, we experience it all as life reveals itself continuously. We arrive at our desired destination, but the journey can be a complete contrast to what we would have preferred or imagined.

Let me take you to the year 2017. Life was like a delicious cocktail — intoxicating and deeply satisfying. My headspace similar to a beach in Hawaii — sunny, laid back and beautiful. I had it all: a big wedding coming up; lots of parties and holidays to plan; tons of clothes and jewelry to be bought and a beautiful four-bedroom apartment to furnish. My childhood conditioning led me to believe that I was THE happiest person on this planet. After all I had everything that money could buy AND I was getting married. Life couldn't have been better! Little did I know this was the calm before, what turned out to be, the scariest storm of my life.

My marriage ended in less than a year. My parents separated after being together for 38 years. They divorced soon after me. I don't know what bothered me more, my parents' marriage ended, my own broken dreams, or the true nature of life was being revealed. Or was it the fear of what people would think about me or my family.

The illusion of security that I grew up with crumbled right before my eyes. My parents were always my benchmark for a successful marriage and life. In India, divorces are uncommon, and in all my years I have been led to believe that a failed marriage means a failed life. And here I was, dealing with not one but two failed marriages.

I was in the depths of despair. I felt alone, disoriented and anxious. My sense of joy was watered down by the cold slap of reality. My entire world was turning upside down. It felt like a bullet had pierced my heart. My eyes that once sparkled now resembled a vacant home being put up for sale. I felt a deep void inside, and the smile that once lived on my face, now mocked me. I didn't think I could ever recover from this.

I had always dreamt of the perfect fairytale happily ever after. I thought marriage would do the trick, but it did the exact opposite. I didn't even know who I was anymore. I yearned to be introduced to myself.

We are all tested at different points in our lives. What makes us unique is how we respond to these tests. Conditioning can be fatal — condemning everything it doesn't recognize and paralyzing us with unnecessary fear and resentment. Building my whole life around my identity as a daughter and then wife, I lacked the survival techniques to cope with life's hardships. Limiting beliefs such as: there is something wrong with you if you are not willing to stay in a dead relationship, added more fuel to the fire burning within. It was time for some serious unlearning.

After several months feeling sorry for myself, and blaming the whole world for my problems, one morning I woke up and saw a notification from Pinterest. Semi awake, I clicked on a link and the following quote appeared on my phone screen: 'Life is a sequence of births and deaths. Moments are born and moments die. For new experiences to come to light, old ones need to wither away.' For a brief moment, I felt a flicker of joy. Until now I had been so preoccupied with resisting change, I couldn't see the opportunities that came with it. Was life giving me a chance to fulfill my dreams?

Could this be the beginning of a brand new chapter in my life? I had to find out.

This was around the time the world was hit by a global pandemic known as COVID-19. Once again, change was in the air. The world was in a complete lockdown. Some days I felt blessed, after all, the world had come to a startling halt, and I could use this time to heal. Other days I felt restless because I couldn't meet anyone. I was thankful that at least I had the company of my mother whom I live with. I could have never imagined that this new 'disaster' would be the answer to my prayers. It was time to create my fairytale.

With nothing to do and nowhere to go, I signed up for an online course on The Science of Happiness. I figured I could learn a thing or two. Week after week, I studied the material, incorporated the teachings into my life and started to feel significantly better. After a long time, I felt a sense of achievement when I completed the course with a whopping 98% on the exam. Not having been the academic type, this was a pleasant surprise. As Joy began crawling back into my life, I sensed I was on a path and needed to take the next step.

A dear family friend of mine, Puja — a successful life coach in the Southern part of India, once told me that I had all the skills required to help others. I reached out to her for some clarity and the next thing I knew, I was enrolled in America's Number one success coach, Jack Canfield's, Train the Trainer Online Program. It took me six months to learn and absorb the Success Principles that he taught. During this training, I felt my world expand. As I started to allow my curiosity to replace my conditioning, life got easier. Like an innocent child excitedly exploring her environment, I started to embrace all experiences as a wise teacher. I stopped labeling people and situations as 'good', 'bad', 'right', and 'wrong'. I started taking 100% responsibility for my life and stopped blaming others. It was during this time that I knew I wanted to spend the rest of my life empowering and uplifting people. If I could get out of the dark hole I was in, then I could help others do the same.

I was in action mode, and the universe decided to reward me. This precious gift came in the form of a highly renowned institute in Canada, offering online programs for people like me, interested in pursuing life coaching as a profession. I am still trying to figure out how I stumbled upon this website. I suspect it was divine intervention. I had classes twice a week, and I met people from across the world, without stepping out of my home. This is when some serious healing took place under the guidance, support and love of Mark, the founder of the Institute. He was Godsent, and I don't even know if I believe in God. It was Mark who helped me rip apart all of my limiting beliefs and enabled me to transform into a powerful being.

Living under the guidance of Jack's Success Principles and Mark's process of self-actualization, I felt I had two guardian angels by my side. I started to look forward to the things that had previously frightened me.

The Universe finally granted me my wish. I found my calling in life, to empower people to create the life of their dreams. I am good at something. I am making a difference. I jump out of bed every morning with child-like enthusiasm. I laugh every single day and feel extremely loved and cherished. With joy as my constant companion, there isn't a single belief strong enough to keep me in a cage anymore.

The journey from entitlement to joy tested me at every step and continues to do so. A path paved with blind spots, speed breakers and U-turns; I've had to continuously challenge my beliefs; question my perceptions; and deconstruct my conditioning. Being kicked out of my comfort zone was a small price to pay. For me, it is a signal that great things are about to happen.

I look back at my life and realize the past is merely a perception, and the future, an illusion. It's the present moment that contains the power of creation. My actions today will bear fruit tomorrow. But then again, there is no tomorrow. It's always today. I ask myself one question, "What can I do today?"

As I sit at my desk in my second-floor home office, looking at my certificates on the wall, I feel proud and excited. One year ago, I was drifting like an aimless boat that had been abandoned at shore. Now my schedule is booked out for the next six months, every single day filled with activities that bring me immense joy. From coaching clients, to conducting online workshops, from writing a chapter in this book, to preparing for my first TEDx talk — I have come a long way. I never thought that such transformation was possible in only one year. Maybe the journey isn't about learning as much as unlearning everything that blocks joy from our lives.

I sit here today, grateful and joyful, for everything I've been given, and for all that I've been denied.

Cherylanne Thomas

❀

Cherylanne has received her MBA and several certifications focused in the area of Sales, Executive Coaching and Leadership Development. She serves as a joyful senior sales and marketing executive and is a lifelong learner. For the past 25 years, with curiosity and passion to elevate sales and leadership teams to a higher level of performance, Cherylanne has transformed many organizations toward greater success by discovering what works to generate an increase in topline revenue. It is her opinion that everything exists for the purpose of joy, and everyone can possess the passion, heart, and desire to share and experience it. Cherylanne is the author of several white papers and resides in the Metro D.C. area.

Contact
Website: www.heartofjoyfulselling.com

The Heart of Joyful Selling

By Cherylanne Thomas

"I define joy as a sustained sense of well-being and internal peace; a connection to what matters."

— Oprah Winfrey

I was nine years old when I started my sales career and I have never-looked backed. Yes, there have been some hills and valleys along the decades, but at nine years old, I knew I had a calling. I didn't know it then, but as newspaper delivery provider, I began to learn the lessons of sales prospecting, building relationships, handling complaints, overcoming objections and running my own business.

I always had a sense of joy and a connection to what matters when I delivered newspapers. I was connecting people to the world in print and it brought me joy. The news I delivered to 56 families, seven days a week, was relevant and whether it was good or bad, it made a difference to their lives.

This chapter is not meant to share sales techniques and principles, but rather depicts a professional sales career as a spiritual calling of care that brings about joy regardless of any religious sector.

The Miriam Webster definition of sales is "to give up (property) to another for something of value (such as money)." It is my opinion that this definition appears sterile and doesn't do justice to the overall human interaction encounter. The art of sales becomes the understanding that "getting is the giving of joy."

I believe that being curious about people and their lives leads to a joyful life. To me, master the art of selling and you master the art of joy. Even if you don't make a sale, there is still joy because you gave value and have become a connection to a cause in the matter for someone.

Sales is about creating the experience of a "one to one" purposeful relationship that sparks something magical when you can stay in conversation. To come from this place, you must think in terms of giving; not getting. Offer value to the purpose and that will serve to bring you joy. The more ways you begin to truly serve people the better chance you have at earning their business. Through the discovery of this process, the customer is privileged with the involvement of you.

As a young adult, I chose a hospitality sales career to express myself and offer joy. To me, it was the ultimate calling of what I was meant to do. I view hospitality as an act of a higher spiritual behavior. Hospitality was regarded by most nations of the ancient world as one of life's chief virtues. I would like to believe this context still exists today. As a hospitality sales professional, I have successfully led many teams to generate millions of dollars for hotel owners by bringing joy to event planners, brides and grooms, and individual guests. As a result, I believe hospitality serves as a virtue that greatly cares for the whole universe through the ties of humanity. Hospitality also plays a fundamental role to augment and increase the volume of sales of an organization. Hence every business should master the art of serving to bring joy to the internal associates and external prospects and clients. The sales professional should know and understand that selling is a service that brings joy into the sales process.

It is my belief there is a correlation between being a great sales person and living life as a great citizen in our world. I remember one day I was with a friend who needed vacuum bags for his vacuum cleaner. We whisked away to a nearby authorized dealer store. We walked into a 750 square foot store and was immediately greeted by a young man, who was ready to serve us. Sales people come in all shapes and sizes. The man that greeted us was short and zaftig and possessed the most joyful and quiet, minded spirit. We weren't there to buy a vacuum cleaner and we made that clear so he didn't have to waste his time with us. On the contrary, the sales professional stated he was there to serve us and asked what type of vacuum cleaner my friend owned. The gentleman left the room and came back with two types of vacuum bags, taking great care of explaining the difference between the two and why he recommended one over the other; which, by the way, wasn't the more expensive vacuum bag of the two he selected. The sales person went on to ask how my friend enjoyed using his vacuum cleaner. My friend made the comment he only knew how to turn it "on and off" and didn't understand the features at all. It was then when the young man said, "Let me go through the features with you so that you can maximize the use of your vacuum cleaner." For the next forty five minutes, this young man took great care in explaining the features and benefits of the vacuum cleaner knowing my friend did not buy the vacuum cleaner from his store. It was an amazing experience because this young man cared for us with such a joyful spirit. For him, it wasn't about the sale it was about the experience of care we received as a customer of the store. I have never forgotten this experience or the young man. It was a magical encounter that still brings me great joy upon reflection.

Sellers can have an impact on a customer's life. They can provide an experience filled to the brim with happiness and joy that can raise consciousness and overflow to an individual's mind and spirit. There are only two types of feelings: good and bad. Indifference also exists but is the kiss of death in my opinion. Thoughts of joy exist in the present state of mind. Don't rob yourself of this gift. Give yourself the opportunity to live a full life of happiness and joy.

As a seller, prospecting brings more joy because it increases the opportunity to make great things happen for someone. A true seller understands a sales career is 24/7. Like caring for a home, there is always something to do. Sales is similar, because there is always one more person we can contact. Everyone is a prospect, now it's our job to qualify that individual as a customer and then as a client. When this is understood, the power of making great things happen is up to us. We get to choose. The power is within us like a beam of light coming from the sun. Choosing to see the light is a metaphor for bringing joy into your heart. It is a choice to bring joy into your life for yourself and others. I ask you to choose well; choose joy. 🏵

Notes

Nancy Carlson

———— ❁ ————

Nancy Carlson is a happy and healthy successful entrepreneur. She is a professional ski instructor and has been a licensed massage therapist for over 30 years. Nancy also enjoys her volunteer time with several community organizations.

Together with her husband, she purchased and renovated a Victorian home into a bed & breakfast, which she ran for 15 years. During that time, she also purchased and continues to run a very busy restaurant. Five years ago she started a Farm to Table Market, which has been incredibly successful, supporting over 25 local farms and artisans. Nancy and her staff prepare and sell soups, salads, sandwiches, entrees, side dishes, and assorted desserts. They also offer catering services.

Nancy and her husband now live in a home they designed and had built on a large lot in the lovely mountains of New Hampshire, and she lives by the mantra: "Joy is a choice and joy is contagious."

Joy is a
Contagious Choice

By Nancy Carlson

*"We cannot cure the world of sorrows,
but we can choose to live in joy."*

— Joseph Campbell

My life started with many challenges. Born the seventh child in my family, only 11 months after a sister, my mother's womb had not recovered. I was a scrawny and sickly child. I suffered through pneumonia five times by the time I was seven years old. My sister said that I stole all the attention.

"You stole all my nutrients," I responded.

Everyone in life has difficulties, so it is a good rule of thumb to refrain from being judgmental of others. It is how we react to our challenges that will determine our outcome.

I, like many young girls was molested. I was emotionally and verbally abused by family members. Distracted at school, it was suggested that I see a counselor. The counselor wanted to meet with as many family members as possible who would contribute an hour on a Saturday for this purpose. The counselor determined that I was the family scapegoat.

I think it was at that time when I learned about choice.

I could either play a victim or make changes in myself that would create better outcomes for me in my life.

On one occasion, I remembered being driven home after babysitting when the driver realized she was too impaired to drive. She decided to take me to my sister's house rather than take the longer drive home. She hit the phone pole in front of my sister's house. I went through the windshield and was hospitalized for several days. My mother gave the hospital permission over the phone to treat my injuries. My sister and her boyfriend went to the hospital with me in the ambulance. My mother did not visit me until my third day in the hospital on her way to work. My father did not visit until he picked me up for my discharge. Following this incident, I felt abandoned and began to rely on friends for attention. Unfortunately, the friends turned out to be the 'wrong crowd' who dabbled with drugs and alcohol. At one point, I wondered if life was worth living and attempted suicide by ingesting many pills. I was not making good choices regarding relationships in my life either. I could go on and on with the challenges that I faced, but that is not how I chose to live my life.

Every young person deserves an adult who will love them unconditionally. For me that person was a neighbor who was supportive with guidelines and yet let me express myself.

In my life's journey, I found people who have encouraged and supported me. There are people with illnesses and hardships who are positive and live life to the fullest. There are also people who complain and blame other people for every tiny challenge in their lives. From these folks, I have learned to make positive choices in life. These choices have allowed me to live life with positivity.

I choose to spend time with like-minded people. This causes the positive energy to spread.

Although I did not attend a formal college, I took various community college courses that interested me as I started making other good choices. I met a wonderful man. He was good clean fun, driven and wanted 'more' out of life. I paid off credit card debt and began saving money. I now wanted an abundance of good things in my life. I learned to set goals. I set a mantra of 'Dream/Believe/Achieve.'

I took a course at the community college 'Introduction to Massage Therapy.' It was then that I realized how much I enjoyed helping others feel better. I also took training in Reiki, an energetic healing modality. I knew I was now on the right track and realized that joy is a choice. I chose to continue my education in massage and have been a Licensed Massage Therapist for over 30 years.

With this wonderful man, I spent weekends in the mountains of New Hampshire, skiing in the winter and living the lake life in the summer. We dreamed of owning a home and running a Bed & Breakfast. We looked at real estate. We explored the area looking at homes, traveling and staying at B&B's. We finally made an offer on a big old farmhouse but were disappointed that it did not materialize. A year later we found another property we thought would work. Again, we were disappointed that it did not materialize. Another year went by, and we finally purchased a Victorian home on a lake with four bedrooms and one bathroom. It needed a lot of attention and we gave it hard work and love. We remodeled it to include six bedrooms and seven bathrooms. We opened and ran it as a B&B for 12 years.

During that time, we got married. My husband managed a restaurant and had dreams of owning his own. Being driven and goal oriented, we purchased a busy successful restaurant which we have been running for over 20 years. Additionally, we have owned and operated a Farm-to-Table Market that has supported over 25 local farms and producers of goods. In time, we purchased a large parcel of land and built a small, beautiful home. It was time to sell the big house on the lake as we had not worked it as a B&B for many years.

Realizing the importance of community and the joy of volunteering, I joined the local garden club. My husband and I enjoy skiing, so we volunteered with the local school to teach kids to ski. This has led us to becoming professional ski instructors. Also, we have served on multiple non-profit boards.

I have learned to set goals, big ones and then, 'Go for It.' I have chosen to live in JOY. I could go on and on about struggles, however I choose to focus on the positive.

I have a sign hanging in my office that reads, "Never be defined by your past. It was a lesson not a life sentence."

It is a choice.

I choose to surround myself with positive people and healthy relationships. I do not regret what I have experienced, even the difficult challenges — the challenges have shaped who I am today. 🏵

Notes

Grace Rosales

Grace Rosales is a Certified Trainer in the Success Principles and a Canfield Certified Trainer. Grace is also certified in Barrett Values — Leadership and Coaching. She incorporates this training in her personal life and as a success coach for women professionals to help them reach their goals and dreams and live a happy, fulfilling life.

Grace is also a legal professional with over 25 years' experence. She currently works in Business Development, Marketing and Competitive Intelligence for a large AmLaw 100 law firm in Los Angeles.

Grace has a Juris Doctor (JD) from Whittier Law School, paralegal degree from UCLA, BA from CSULB in Speech Communications and a Masters in Library and Information Sciences (MLIS) from the University of North Texas.

Grace lives with her significant other, Daniel in Marina del Rey, CA along with their 2 lovable labs, Fred and Lucy. She loves to run on the beach and is currently training for the Los Angeles Marathon.

Contact

Website: www.gracerosales.com

My Left Foot

By Grace Rosales

"If you carry joy in your heart, you can heal any moment."

— Carlos Santana

Have you ever worked so hard for something only to have it go wrong in the last possible minute? And when that unimaginable, unexpected thing happens, can you still find joy in it?

This is the story of my left foot.

I was putting on the biggest event of my life at my law firm — an office opening — with the most important people from all over the country flying in. It had to be perfect. The pressure was on.

A few hours before the event, I was walking back from lunch with my work colleagues when the unthinkable happened. I missed a step and fell forward, almost hitting my head on the ground. Luckily, I was able to stop myself from rolling over using both hands. This all happened in front of many people in the middle of a busy office courtyard. Slowly, I tried to get up from this embarrassing fall and quickly wiped the dirt from my arms, knees and dress that I wore that day. I noticed several scratches but no blood- thank goodness. But when I attempted to take that first step, I noticed to my horror that I was not able to walk on my left foot.

The pain was quickly becoming unbearable.

I'm sure all my work colleagues were worried for me that day. But instead of worrying about my own pain all I could think about was not wanting THEM to worry. I remember looking at my boss straight in the eye and telling her 'I'll be back' in time for the event.

I couldn't imagine missing it. I had worked so hard on this.

I was immediately rushed to a nearby hospital. While waiting for my x-ray results, I tried to comprehend what just happened. I kept asking myself, 'Did this really happen? How is this even possible? I work out every day!' Then my mind shifted to: 'There is no way I will miss this event. I will be there on crutches, if I need to. It's going to be awesome.'

As I was contemplating this, I looked at the three very concerned co-workers who witnessed my embarrassing fall and accompanied me to the hospital. They became my support team for that day. One co-worker gave me a piggy-back ride to the doctor's office since I couldn't walk. Another co-worker carried my belongings. A third co-worker provided some comic relief and took silly pictures of me. They all could have gone back to the office but they chose to stay with me so I wouldn't be alone.

Even during that humiliating moment, I chose joy and gratitude. I felt grateful that my co-workers were with me during those scary moments. I felt joy as they cheered me on while I was learning to use crutches and a walking boot for the first time in my life so I could return to my event. We laughed together as I got another piggy-back ride to the office while smiling and waving at everyone who was staring oddly at us. I felt relieved and lucky that I was able to get back and actually attend my incredible event.

On that fateful day, I somehow found the courage to choose joy and that helped ease the pain of my injured left foot.

When the MRI results came back, it showed that I had broken all the bones in my left foot. All this happened from missing one step. I broke down and cried in disbelief. I was told that I needed to have a special foot surgery immediately, called Lisfranc surgery, which was not the usual. It is the most uncommon and severe injury one can sustain in one's foot. It happens to 1 of 50,000-60,000 people annually. My doctor said the surgery had to be done within the month of my accident or my condition would worsen. Additionally, he said that even if the surgery and healing went well, I still might never be able to run again. How could I be so lucky?

Things went further downhill from there. During my pre-op exam my doctor discovered an undetected heart condition — an atrial flutter (a type of abnormal heart rhythm, or arrhythmia). My heart was beating too fast. Normal heart rate is between 60-100 bpm. Mine was over 120 at the time just from sitting down. I retook the EKG test a few times and got the same dismal results. Because of this, they couldn't clear me for surgery. My heart sank. Not only was I scared I may never run again, but now I had to worry about having a stroke.

I was sent to a cardiologist immediately who prescribed drugs to help lower my heart rate. When those didn't work, I was sent to another cardiology specialist for a consultation. I was seeing doctors several times a week and dreaded that because nothing seemed to work and my deadline for surgery was quickly approaching.

I felt my health deteriorating from all the stress and I couldn't sleep at night due to my rapid heart rate. I was losing more weight, already under 95 lbs. There were many times I thought I was going to die.

'Is this it for me?' All this was happening while my significant other, Daniel, was working in India. I felt alone, scared, stressed out and angry at myself for allowing this to happen. This was a very low point of my life.

As a last resort the cardiology specialist scheduled a 'cardioversion' to be performed immediately. This involves restarting your heart by sending electric shocks to your heart to restore a normal heart rhythm. After the 'cardioversion' I was able to schedule a new surgery date — one day shy of my one-month deadline. Thank goodness.

My Lisfranc surgery was a success. I now have nine screws and two metal plates in my left foot. I needed to be off my feet for several months and learn to balance on one foot. Imagine trying to balance on one foot, in crutches, in a 2-story house, with two large Labrador Retrievers with me at home alone.

I have never felt more challenged in my life.

I was in excruciating pain for the first few weeks especially at night. I would awaken to a sharp throbbing pain like my foot was being squeezed in a vice. They gave me Oxy and hydrocodone which made me dizzy and nauseated so I stopped taking it. I only used Tylenol Extra Strength which wasn't as strong. I would often lay awake in tears praying the pain would end soon.

Even worse, I went online to research Lisfranc surgery recovery, and it was depressing because people who had my surgery had terrible outcomes. I was in a lot of pain, felt helpless and discouraged. I was flooded with thoughts that I may never walk the same again. This was a death sentence for me. I loved to work out and walk my dogs daily. Yet even during those dark moments, somehow, I kept thinking this was all happening for a reason.

'Something good was going to come out of this.'

Then one day I noticed a book, "The Success Principles — How to Get to Where You Are to Where You Want To Be" by Jack Canfield. I started reading it every day. It was exactly what I needed, and I started applying the principles to my life.

I began visualizing that I could run with my dogs, Fred and Lucy, that I could work out, that I could run that 5K charity run again. I set goals and created affirmations. It was summer. I made my goal to walk Fred and Lucy and work out before the end of the year.

I changed my limiting beliefs about my left foot and started to find a way to work out every day so I could become stronger sooner. I found non-weight bearing exercises on YouTube and modified chair and floor workouts to stay strong and sane. I downloaded a meditation app, Calm, and started 10-minute guided meditations every day. I turned to motivational reading which was very uplifting. I replaced watching the evening news with funny movies and animal shows. I chose bright colored cast covers to dress up my cast to put me in a good mood. I started trying new recipes and learned to be a better cook and baker. I even shared my book with my friends who saw how much it was helping me.

Choosing to do things that made me happy had a profound effect on my recovery. As a result, I was able to recover faster. My surgeon said, 'I was one of his best healers!'

In less than four months I was able to walk with my dogs and return to work. In less than five months I was able to go spinning again. In less than eight months, I successfully ran the 'Run for Justice 5K' with only two minutes longer than my personal best!

I told the good news to my surgeon. He called me a 'rock star.' I'll take it! Now I work out every day and run several times a week. During each run, I repeat to myself, 'I love you left foot.' At 54, I'm actually in the best shape of my life.

During the pandemic I started visualizing longer runs, saying positive affirmations and posting them everywhere. I signed up for nutrition and running programs to grow stronger and run longer. I started sharing my goals with family and friends.

It was slightly less than a year ago that my big goal was to run a half marathon by December 2021. I have surpassed that. I completed 19 miles last February. To think the furthest I had run was three miles a year ago. And this year, I have registered to run the LA Marathon!

By getting myself out of victim mode and shifting my belief and changing the stories that I told myself I was able to get the outcome I wanted and achieve even more. It made me realize anything is possible if you change your mindset, decide what you want and really go after your goals.

Looking back, I kept thinking that this was all happening for a reason. I may not know what that reason is, but I knew I had to keep a positive mindset. I had to keep going no matter what.

Now when I look at my left foot every day I smile with pride. Even though I wake up with stiffness in my left foot every day, I choose joy.

My left foot is consistently a reminder of joy.

Even though I have this heart condition I am still choosing joy. Every day I put an oil called "Joy" on my heart. It is a reminder that there is so much to be grateful for every day.

Every day I remember to give myself grace, not just because my name is Grace. I remember to show compassion and kindness to myself even when things do not seem perfect. It is about loving myself unconditionally because I did the best I could. Thinking this way brings me comfort and joy.

So, what's your left foot? What do you need to heal from? What are you telling yourself that you can't do? We all have crutches that we hobble around on in life. Whatever it is, you don't have to be stuck. You can shift your mindset, choose joy and live the life that you really want.

I invite you to choose joy today and every day. May you always find love in your life and peace in your heart. 🌸

Rev. Gayle Dillon

❀

She began her business career in the telecommunications industry at age 18. She retired at 48 and needed to keep working because of poor life choices. At age 50 she began to wonder: is this is good as it gets?

Today, Gayle is an Ordained Minister with Centers for Spiritual Living. She is also a Certified Canfield Trainer in the Success Principles. She received her Masters Degree in Consciousness Studies from the Holmes Institute.

Gayle is using her Canfield and Rayner Institute training plus all her life experience to create her own coaching business, Practical Everyday Wisdom. She is passionate about inspiring people in recovery to fearlessly live their best lives so that they experience a new level of belonging. Gayle helps people awaken to their best selves.

Gayle is a mother of two, grandmother of nine and now happily married to Paul. She is currently moving from Kent, WA to Ocean Park, WA.

Contact

Website: www.practicaleverydaywisdom.com
Email: gayle@practicaleverydaywisdom

Messed Up to Blessed Up

By Rev. Gayle Dillon

"Joy; the kind of happiness that doesn't depend on what happens."

— David Steindl-Rast

My best friend died at 15 and it was my fault. She died of leukemia, and I believed I caused it, crazy as that sounds. This became a defining moment for me; a factor that played heavily in my life for years to come.

For the first 50 years of my life, I felt worthless. When I was young, I was told that I was an accident, I was told I wouldn't live past 30 days, and if I did, I'd be a vegetable and blind by the time I was 6. Not a great start for building self-esteem.

It usually takes a whole bunch of small events and decisions to change your life. Yet, when you recognize that your life has changed, it seems like it happened in an instant.

"If you don't change your life you're going to die or you're going to kill someone." How the hell did I get here? I didn't know whose voice it was and yet I knew it was true . . . the jig was up.

But wait, I'm getting ahead of myself, let's take a walk down memory lane.

I grew up in the Pacific Northwest, 30 miles east of Seattle in a small town of 900 people. My parents moved there when I was 2. My sister was 10 and my brother was 14 when they were pulled out of their city school and thrown into small town USA. I can't imagine how that move changed their lives or my parents' lives.

I don't believe my childhood was filled with any more trauma than most kids growing up in the 50's and 60's. I was lucky really. My parents didn't fight; my brother and sister weren't mean to me and yet something always seemed out of balance.

When I was 15 my first personal trauma happened; Cass (my best friend) died of leukemia. The year before we had been at the ocean riding motorcycles in the surf, it was fun and cold. When they first diagnosed her with leukemia the doctor told her mother he believed that cancers lie dormant in all of us until there is a shock to our system which makes the cancer come alive (oh my God, the cold ocean water!). Consequently, I believed that I was responsible for her getting leukemia and ultimately dying from the disease.

The pain, anger, hurt and guilt were so consuming that at the ripe age of 15, I learned how to anesthetize myself with nicotine, alcohol, and drugs.

The first time I drank and smoked I drank myself into a blackout and had hallucinations about Cass. For some pervasive reason it also gave me a sense of confidence. I felt bold and courageous and indestructible. Which is really a joke, since I was on a self-imposed path of destruction.

I was a junior in high school and 17 years old when I found out I was pregnant. This was not my first sexual encounter. My parents didn't want me to have the baby, but I believed the father loved me, so I packed up my things and moved in with his family. It was odd that he had an apartment and I living at his mom's house. Long story short: I had a miscarriage . . . relationship over. I found myself living in the projects alone and scared with a woman I really didn't know that well. She must have sensed I was truly out of my element and called my parents. My dad immediately came and picked me up. I think she was my first guardian angel. A guardian angel is defined as a spirit that is believed to watch over and protect a person or place. I believe guardian angels come in human form too, at least they have in my life.

When you don't have any self-worth, you tend to attract people into your life that get their self-worth through abuse. So, of course, I was attracted to misogynistic men. My first real relationship moved quickly into full on physical abuse. He made promises, let other women pay for the privilege of spending time with him and then came home to me. When I finally got tired of the cheating instead of just leaving, I thought 'an eye for an eye'. The only difference was I could and did get pregnant from my one-night stand. My son was a godsend in many ways and to protect him I found the courage to leave. My son is my second guardian angel. While my abuser was at work, I packed the two of us up in my car and moved back home to my parents. I had dodged another bullet and yet I was still lost.

I was really good at advancing my career which meant more money to spend but it's hard to fill a hole of emptiness. It really doesn't matter if its drugs, alcohol, cigarettes, sex or credit cards; if you're not happy and you don't know how to be happy, all you're really doing is hoping that the next "thing" will fill the void.

The next guy I met in a bar asked me to move in with him. I really thought I had broken the cycle and life would be different. We even had a child together. Although he was a doting father to his son, he was emotionally abusive to my older son and to me. He was never physically abusive and sometimes emotional abuse is far more insidious. It took me a while to realize he was not faithful. Again, instead of leaving, I decided, two can play that game and I had an affair with a married man. My life, my choice. BAD CHOICE. I ended up leaving and moving back in with my parents, again.

At this point, I now had two boys by two different men, never married and not yet 30. I am as messed up as the men I attracted. I never believed I was a victim, but I did allow myself to be victimized.

I got into another relationship where the physical abuse escalated and so did the drugs and alcohol. In January 1989, I came home from work and found my house literally surrounded by police cars. My first thought was "run", my second was "what the hell are they doing in my house?" and my third thought was dread and recognition. I was arrested for possession with intent to distribute. They were partly right. I used to get so high I would beseech God that if I did not die, I would quit. I would always pull through and then not keep my end of the bargain. This went on nightly. Today I honestly believe if I had not been arrested, I eventually would have overdosed; I have always believed my prayer was answered. The people who called the cops were my third guardian angels.

This was an opportunity to re-focus and start over. I went to treatment once a week, attended two AA meetings a week, consulted with a therapist and went to church every Sunday. I finally ended this abusive marriage BUT I did not change my beliefs about myself, nor did I change my friends.

When I moved out and bought a house on my own, I believed my life had turned a corner. Then one night, "THE" incident happened; something that brought me to my knees in shame. I went out with a girlfriend who like me had an appetite for self-destruction. We were taking college classes together and were both 20-25 years older than the rest of the students. We went to a party that some of the students were throwing. We walked in and started doing shots of tequila and smoking pot. I immediately blacked out. I remember walking to a park with a young man and sitting on a picnic table. Later, I woke up in bed with a couple having no idea how I got there. Even though I was fully clothed, I was horrified. I literally dropped out of school. And that's when I heard the voice:

"If you don't change your life you're going to die or you're going to kill someone."

My life had been screaming at me and I wasn't paying attention! I was ready to release myself from this trap of self-destruction. I had to deal with all my negative self-talk. I was desperate to find myself, to maybe even like myself. This time I not only listened; I took action and responsibility to change my life. My Life, My Choice; GOOD CHOICE!

It didn't happen overnight but one Sunday I walked into a Centers for Spiritual Living where their motto is "Change Your Thinking, Change Your Life" and I thought, HELL YES! I can think and I can change. Why not me? This was my path out of hell. This was for me. This was my lifeline.

If you had told me that my entire life was going to change tomorrow, that someday I would become Rev. Gayle, that someday I would lead a Centers for Spiritual Living community of my own; I would have thought...what are you smoking?? Evidently there was a bigger plan for my life than even I was aware of because it all came true.

Today, I am married to a wonderful man that doesn't have an abusive bone in his body. We have been together since 2003. I still confront insecurities. What I won't and don't do is give up ME to make anyone else happy and neither does he. I have learned to love and respect myself. I have learned to look at every situation in my life and ask: what part am I playing in this play today? I always have a choice.

Life happens to all of us; it's how we react to what we have been dealt that helps us to heal or keeps us stuck. I can't change my past. Each and every day I am given the opportunity to be the best me I can be. Sometimes I knock it out of the park and other times I strike out swinging. What I do know is I am always in the game.

I believe each one of us has opportunities in our life to change — in fact I really believe we are given these opportunities daily. It took me 50 years to begin to believe that I have a purpose and drugs and alcohol kept me anesthetized from living my life to the fullest. My passion now is providing people with the tools to make the necessary changes in their lives. No one can do it for us. We individually have to decide we are worth it.

YOU ARE A MIRACLE. Scientists estimate the odds of your being born at about one in 400 trillion. Think about that — one in 400 trillion. Against all odds, you are here. You are not a mistake. You are not bad. You are not unworthy. Yes, the odds might be stacked against you and life might appear tough, but you can do it. It is your life and it is your choice.

"And tell me what it is that you see
A world that's full of endless possibilities
And heroes don't look like they used to
They look like you do"
The Alternate Routes, Nothing More ❀

Jennie Ritchie

❀

Jennie Is a Certified Canfield Trainer in the Success Principles and a Mindset, Action & Accountability coach for women in Network Marketing and Direct Selling. She taught middle and high school for 25 years, but after authoring the Amazon best-selling book: *Keeping it Together When Life Throws You Curves*, Jennie realized coaching was her passion.

Jennie is an expert in translating personal development principles into real-world language for audiences worldwide. She is passionate about helping women achieve their business and personal goals by recognizing their own potential and overcoming obstacles. No matter where you are, or where you've been, Jennie can help you believe in yourself and remember that anything is possible.

Jennie is a mother of three, grandmother to one and happily 'empty nesting' in Newport Beach with her husband.

Contact

Website: www.jennieritchie.com

Choosing Joy at Sunset

By Jennie Ritchie

"Find out where joy resides and give it a voice far beyond singing, for to miss the joy is to miss all."

— Robert Louis Stevenson

It was one of those crazy nights, one where my husband and I were racing home from work in order to get ourselves and our youngest daughter, Rachel, to her volleyball school opening banquet. We had just moved back to Southern California, and this was late summer, so she hadn't started at her new school yet. Although she wanted to make the move, this new school meant higher expectations, different pressures and zero friends. It was a stressful time for her. She was unsure about where she fit in and being one of the oldest on her team, she didn't have a lot in common with the other girls. We arrived at the banquet and she did her best to socialize with the girls, but it was awkward to say the least. As parents, we listened to the information about the season and fundraising requirements and enjoyed meeting other parents and coaches.

As we began the ride home, Rachel was sitting in the backseat, silent and on her phone. Though she had a happy face at the banquet, that quickly disappeared, and she was basically in her own world, answering my questions curtly. I felt like she was being somewhat disrespectful. Looking back, I know that this was how she was handling her stress and anxiety. However, at the time, I got a little defensive . . . reminding her that she should be grateful and that we came to the banquet and how much we do for her. (Not my best "Mom" moment.)

The closer we got to home, the worse I felt and the more irritated I became. Before long, I had worked myself into a fairly negative emotional state. When we pulled up in front of our house, I told my husband I needed to go for a walk. I knew I needed to blow off some steam or the rest of the night was not going to go well.

We live on an island and sunset is my favorite time of day. I knew that if I could see the sunset, I would feel better. I started walking toward the north end of the island, in my jeans and heels, amid the tourists coming back from the beach in their shorts and flip flops.

As a coach, I often guide people through the process of taking stock of their emotions in a given moment. So, at this moment, I asked myself, "Why am I feeling like this? and "Is this how I want it to feel?" It was almost like Dr. Phil asking one of his TV show guests, "How's that working for you?" And, in all honesty, it wasn't working for me. I didn't want to feel like this. I didn't want to feel irritated, annoyed, negative and frustrated.

The next question quickly followed, "How would I rather feel?"

The answer was JOYFUL. I live a blessed and fortunate life and I would rather feel joy.

By that time, I arrived at the sunset and there I wondered to myself, how can I break this down? How would this look more specifically? What emotions could contribute to that feeling of joy? In that moment, four emotions came quickly into my mind: peace, excitement, love, and gratitude.

As I sat there on the cement sea wall watching the sunset, with my feet dangling over the sand, I analyzed each of those emotions one by one.

First, peace. What is peace? Peace is the feeling that everything is going to be alright, that everything is going to work out just as it should. Peace dissolves worry and stress. Peace is calm. Peace trusts. I feel peace from my faith in God, but you might find it in a different higher power or source energy. Peace is allowing the situation to unfold and knowing that all will be well.

Second, excitement. What is excitement? Excitement is looking for-ward with anticipation and hope to the future. It could be excitement about a new relationship, an upcoming weekend event or opportunity, your business and where it's headed, etc. You might feel excitement about the fact that you're making a bigger difference in the world. Excitement is looking forward to something.

Third is love. Love always brings an amazing feeling because it ex-pands the heart. Love doesn't judge. Love appreciates people and allows them to exist as they are. As I sat there, I thought of different types of love and love for different things. Love for God. Love of nature. Love for others in the world. Love for myself, my husband, my daughter and our other children and family. Love melts away differences. It doesn't come from any place of judgement. Love illuminates our similarities. It is em-pathetic, looking for reasons to appreciate others instead of becoming irritated with them.

Fourth is gratitude. Gratitude has always been a powerful force in my life. When I can create a grateful space, my mood immediately shifts to the positive. Gratitude flips a switch inside of me, shifting my focus to an appreciation of my surroundings, my blessings and everything I have. It shrinks challenges, or the perception of challenges, because one is focused on good things. In a difficult moment, if I can call up even a small feeling of gratitude, I am able to feel a bit of positivity, which can end the pity party.

By the time the sun disappeared below the horizon, I felt much bet-ter. I walked back to my family as a different person; more like the person they wanted to be around, a person who wanted to be around them. I am so grateful for the experience I had that night. Now, every chance I get, I walk or ride my bike down to the end of the island, take deep breaths and go through my four special emotions, focusing on each one at a time, thinking thoughts that bring feelings of peace, love, ex-citement, and gratitude. I have also learned to apply my essential oils as a way to refocus, calm, and reset my mind. These tools work a miracle inside me every time.

So how do you want to feel? Do you want to feel hopeful, rejuvenat-ed, satisfied or empowered? You can feel how you want to feel. You can feel joy.

It's a simple, yet magical process . . . as long as you're honest with yourself. Ask yourself the following questions:

- What are you feeling?
- Why are you feeling that way?
- Is that what you want to be feeling?
- If not, how you would rather feel?

Have you worked through this type of activity before? If so, what kind of answers have you received? If not, I invite you to try the process for yourself. It can be tough in the beginning, but the more you do it, the more you learn to really hear and trust yourself. Give yourself permission to feel how you are feeling. Are you feeling disappointed, small, invisible, frustrated, judged? There are lots of feelings. Try not to judge yourself at this moment. Those feelings aren't bad. It's OK to feel the way you're feeling. The question is, "Would you rather feel differently? And if so, how would you rather feel?"

You can feel differently. It's true. Because of this fact: you can change your feelings . . . just like I did on my way to the sunset that night. Our external circumstances don't have to control how we feel.

For example, if you put two different people in the same situation, they won't necessarily react the same. What if your husband comes home every day after work and promptly plops right down on the couch without even giving you a "hello"? If two different people experienced this situation, one might react with annoyance while the other could react with empathy.

We can choose how we feel in a certain situation.

How? By remembering that feelings come from thought. If we can change our thoughts (and there is a ton of research proving that we can), we can change our emotions. So, decide how you want to feel and become intentional about choosing thoughts that create those emotions. Even though it sounds simple, it does take work . . . but it is possible with practice.

As I've made my visits to the sunset and becoming intentional about my emotions a regular practice in my life, it has made a difference for me in so many ways, and mainly these three:

First, it forces me to pause. I physically take a few big, long deep breaths, which automatically slows my mind and body. We run such a fast-paced life and there are proven mental, emotional, and physical benefits to pausing. I feel my stress level decrease, my shoulders relax and my mind calms down.

Second, it helps me remember that there is something bigger than me. It shrinks the challenges of the day into their proper place while widening my perspective; reminding me that things usually work out . . . and what's really important in my life. I may have just been feeling like a new challenge is daunting and wondering how I'll ever solve it . . . and when I see the sunset, I feel like I can tackle it one step at a time.

Third, it reminds me that I get to choose. I am not captive or prisoner to what is happening in the moment. I can choose. I can say no. I can make a different decision and turn it around. I can change how I'm feeling and that is so powerful.

Decide how you want to feel. Focus on a few emotions that will help you feel joy and the thoughts that will bring those emotions. Then practice thinking those thoughts as often as you can. When a situation comes up where you are not feeling the way you want to, consciously call upon the desired thoughts and feelings and apply your essential oils too. I believe in you. It can be done. Choose to make a different decision . . . Choose joy.

JAN FRASER INSPIRED LIFE SERIES

Living

JOY

Dr. Mori Morris-Mitchell

---❁---

Dr. Mori Morris-Mitchell taught social work classes for more than 20 years. She is a highly skilled, self-motivated professional with diverse skills; expertise in training and development, coaching and consulting; skilled with building strategic partnerships to promote forward-thinking leadership to achieve success.

She enjoys inspiring women to dream BIG! When you work with Dr. Mori discover how to reclaim your life, take 100% responsibility, decide what you want, and develop a specific plan to achieve your goals. She welcomes the opportunity to be your personal coach, trainer, and encourager. If you are interested in having her work with you, small or large groups or as a motivational speaker you may contact her on her website below.

Contact
Website: www.drmorimorrismitchell.com

Lessons My Grandparents Taught Me About Joy

By Mori Morris-Mitchell, Ed.D., MPPA, MSW

"Life doesn't have to be perfect to be filled with joy."

— Anonymous

What comes to your mind when you think of the word joy? Do you think of nature? Do you have visions of children rolling down a hill in wide-eyed merriment? Joy is a rather elusive concept, somewhat hard to define, yet important for our mere existence. Joy is hard to ignore because it is a representation of our deeper selves and something more than a positive emotion.

When I think about joy, I don't really think about its meaning. I think about the impact it has on my life. I think about the overwhelming significance of fruit-bearing that evolves from joy and my ability to give it away. In my mind, joy is paramount to breathing. Can you imagine starting your day without a cup of joy? Is it even possible to live a joy-filled life each day, you might ask? It is true, the circumstances of life can wear you down, but it doesn't mean you have to bow to it. I learned early in life how to outsmart joy-robbers from my maternal grandparents Isaac and Anna (Dorcas) Mackey.

Joy-robbers are experiences and activities that delay progress. We have all experienced *joy-robbers* at one time or another. For example, personal attacks made on your character, bullying, and envy. What about self-sabotage? The pain you and I inflict upon ourselves. It undermines your worth and causes you to doubt who you are and what you can truly achieve in life.

I grew up in an era where children were *seen and not heard*. I was aware of my grandparents' love for me by the way they smiled and the affection I received from my grandmother. Nonetheless, I don't recall receiving one-on-one-time with my grandparents. I didn't sit on my grandfather's knee listening to his tales about the good 'ole' days. When my grandmother hugged me, she did not whisper in my ear that I was brilliant and one day I would make my entire family proud. It was understood I was already amazing and ultimately, I would achieve a level of success they had only dreamed about. It was not what my grandparents personally said to me, it was how they lived their lives day in and day out. They modeled life principles: integrity, courage, faith, and persistence. As their granddaughter, I was a student learner and avid observer of the life they lived.

When Grandpa Isaac and Grandma Anna emigrated from Nassau, Bahamas, to the United States little did they know the journey they were about to embark upon would be arduous. My grandfather convinced young Anna to leave her homeland and family to travel to a land of promise and opportunity. Unfortunately, it proved to be more of a promise rather than an opportunity. They were married for 56 years. Together they worked as a team, learned to love each other, and find solace in their God. Raising twelve children, the years were long and hard.

Grandfather built my grandmother a four-bedroom structure that accommodated her needs in the best way possible. We grandkids considered that high living back in those days, although it was still a shack. We never knew the difference because of the love that came from that humble abode. I recall stories about my grandfather picking oranges for fifty cents a day and my grandmother washing and ironing the shirts of well-to-do white men for fifty cents as well. As a child growing up, I don't remember a harsh word ever spoken between them. When my grandfather found more suitable work, he gave my grandmother his paycheck to manage household expenses. They always made sure there was money set aside to tithe and to do whatever was necessary for God's house. This was very important because it was another way to express appreciation and commitment for what God had done for them through the years.

To let them tell it, God had done plenty. They were never hungry. Their children and grandchildren were healthy, thriving, and making significant contributions not only to their own families but to granddaddy and grandmother as well. They had a garden with plenty of vegetables and fruit trees that grew in the backyard. In the front yard, there were huge rose apple and mango trees to sit and rest under on lazy summer days. Under those trees, grandmother would teach her little grandchildren about God and the importance of the Bible.

On a larger scale they taught our entire family about faith, respect for others, the love of family, and community. They embedded into our hearts and memory that blood was thicker than water and a three-fold chord could not easily be broken. What better joy and reward could one have than sacrificing self for family? That's exactly what my grandparents did and the love and joy they imparted still reigns among us today.

They made an indelible imprint on my heart. Here are a few of the guiding principles they taught me about harnessing joy:

Joy Is Measured by One's Heart Not By the Size Of Your Bank Book

We have confused and branded people who do not have money as helpless, joyless, and incapable of achieving goals and success. Some of the richest and happiest people in the world may not have joy. Appearances can be deceiving. My grandparents cautioned me about pointing a finger at those who appear to be *less than*. Nevertheless, their joy bears witness to their generous hearts and love for others which can't be measured in terms of money or material possessions.

Joy Is Transportable

Have you ever observed people at work or when you're traveling? Some wear a furrowed brow on their forehead which may be caused by worry. Others appear to have swallowed a jar of sour pickle juice. If the mere thought of engaging in a friendly conversation causes you to pause; there is an imaginary sign across their chest that reads approach at your own risk. Despite how people may look or the masks they wear, be prepared to share your joy, and show empathy because you will never know when you will need the same kindness returned.

Joy Helps You During the Rough Times

Weeping may endure for a night, but joy cometh in the morning (Psalm 30:5). My grandparents experienced plenty of hardships during their lifetime, including the untimely death of two children. Of course, there were unanswered questions, and even moments of bewilderment. They assured me everyone will experience hardships, no one will be excluded. It is inevitable. They clung to their faith and they truly believed joy was on the way. "You just have to be patient and wait for it". They were right.

Joy Helps You Stay On A Clear Path

Joy is believed to be an inner guidance system. It is an important concept comprised of values and experiences learned that serve to ignite your passion and motivate you on the journey toward success. Anything less than a joy-filled life hampers your purpose and your reason for being. For example, another golden nugget my grandparents shared involved the choosing of friends. They knew if I hung around unsavory people, I could easily be influenced and end up in a place I would later regret. I can clearly hear them say, "birds of a feather, flock together." If you want to stay on a clear path, aspire to do something worthwhile, stay focused, pay attention to those who are moving in the direction you want to go.

Joy Reminds You to Be Grateful

Does it appear as if you are constantly fighting an uphill battle? Is your life overshadowed by difficulties that seem to affect your physical and emotional wellbeing? Then, try making a list of all the things you are grateful for. As you record them you will be amazed at how miniscule your problems will become.

I am grateful for the ordinary things in life — the morning dew, the smell of rain on a Spring day, and freshly cut grass. I don't understand the intricacies of brain functions. The ability to think rational thoughts and participate in pleasant conversations with family and friends is one of the incredible outcomes of a functional brain. And for that I am grateful. I also use my skills in a way to promote peace, to display generosity toward others, and yes, even give away joy. What are you grateful for?

Joy Is Meant To Be Celebrated and Given Away

My grandmother was known for her hospitality. She baked homemade bread for people in the community as a way to connect with friends and help people who were hurting. She said, "It's not how much you get in return but how much you give". If your joy emanates from the heart, others will not only see it but will feel it. Like love, joy has to be celebrated and given away. It's the right thing to do.

Joy is the Loving Creator's Message for You

When you are discouraged, weary, lack confidence, or you get *the big eyes* (want what someone else has), pause for a moment; lift your heart and soul to the Creator who has designed joy specifically for you. Can you feel the warm embrace? Listen intently to what he has to say, as he whispers in a manner only you can understand about how much he loves and cares for you. Don't overlook the caress and the wonderful lessons he wants to teach you on the journey to joy.

These principles of joy helped me understand what it took to persevere and to remain strong despite obstacles, how to serve, believe in myself, show compassion, and trust the Creator. I am still mastering these principles, as I am on the road to understanding my authentic self. I learned that I did not need a high school diploma or a college education to enjoy and spread joy everywhere. I simply had to be myself. By being me, I discovered I already had confidence and everything I needed to reach my goals. I did not believe in those false claims about achieving overnight success. In order to be successful, I knew I had to work, clearly communicate my vision with enthusiasm, and collaborate with others. That meant communicating with real joy and excitement.

If you are disheartened after waiting several years without any results, then your timing may be off, or you may need to revisit your goals to see what is not working. Trust the Joy Process. My grandparents would say,

"Whatever, you're going through is temporary, joy is on the way, just wait for it." They were right.

Points To Ponder

The following questions are for your reading group, family, or friends. Have everyone read the message while answering the questions to understanding the Joy Process.

1. Describe your most favorite joyful moment.
2. Identify 1-2 people who have helped you to understand the meaning of joy. What lessons did you learn from them?
3. Describe how you would like to share joy with others.
4. What do you know about joy now that you wished you had known earlier? 🏵

Notes

Starr Pilmore

❀

Starr is an Author, International speaker and Intuitive Life Coach. She combines several modalities in a unique approach to help others break free from the potholes, bumps, or road-blocks involving our belief system that hold us back from living our dreams.

Following her life-altering bout with cancer, Starr set out on a new journey utilizing her 30 plus years in the medical field as an Air Force Medic and Nurse. She now uses her medical background, intuitive capabilities and Aroma Freedom knowledge to help others along their journey to InJoy.

It is Starr's greatest joy to help others live in a state of joy and alignment with their true purpose.

Starr is passionate in her mission of sparking joy in this world. She believes at her core if we can share and live an "InJoy Life" we can raise the vibration of the planet and realize peace, love, and joy for all who live here.

Contact
Website: www.injoyjourney.com

Joy Compass

By Starr Pilmore, R.N.

"Don't ask what the world needs. Ask what makes you come alive, and go do it. Because what the world needs is people who have come alive."

— Howard Thurman

In 2011, while on this journey called life, I hit a major roadblock called cancer. It was this pause in my journey that allowed me to redirect my course and follow another path. This road was the one that made me "come alive" as I found my calling, purpose, and my true desire. At the time, I thought the vehicle called my body was falling apart; however, it really was just giving me a warning sign it was long overdue for a tune-up and a change of direction.

It was happening so fast after the routine mammogram. The call came in "you need a biopsy", then another call "you need to see a surgeon." All the while no one would answer my question, "Is it cancer?" Being the nurse that I am, I grabbed my biopsy report from medical records on the way to the surgeon.

There it was in black and white, no denying it now. It was a fairly large malignant tumor, and I knew that meant cancer. I felt like all the blood was rushing out of my body and I went numb. I felt frozen in time

119

unaware of the elevator moving. I could barely hear him say, "Ma'am isn't this your floor?" By now the tears were streaming down my face and I ran into the bathroom wanting to throw up. All I could think about is how could this be happening. We have no family history of breast cancer, I am healthy, I don't feel sick.

As I pulled myself together the best I could, the doctor went over my plan. "We need to start chemotherapy immediately," he says, "then afterwards we will do a mastectomy. You can decide then if you want a double mastectomy." Wait! What? I'm fine! I don't feel sick. I'm still on the schedule at work. I can't start now! Next, the oncologist came in to talk with me and the detour through cancer began.

The treatment didn't go as planned. I ended up extremely ill and on a lot of different medications to help with the multitude of side effects I was experiencing. I ended up in the hospital more times than I was at home. At one point I ended up in hospice for palliative care and to better manage the array of symptoms that arose from the chemotherapy. I was at a tipping point in my life as I watched my world crumble before me through the haze of brain fog. I didn't know how I could ever work again, my relationship fell apart, and my financial stability vanished. Along with all the physical pain and discomfort, it also brought up painful childhood wounds that I had never sought help for. It was at this point I just wanted to die; I had given up.

At the lowest point of treatment, a strange thing happened. After a difficult conversation over life and death, I chose to live, and, in that choice, I decided to heal. I decided to follow my heart and live the life I was meant to live. At that moment I had no clue how to do this. Still facing scars from a tumultuous upbringing, I was confused at who or what to turn to. I knew there was some "power to be"; I just didn't identify with the traditional views of God and religion that I grew up with.

That day I asked the Divine to help me. I decided that the "powers to be" were loving and supportive and would help guide my path. So, my healing and path to an 'InJoy' life began that day. Along the way I was guided to use a compass called Joy. It was given with a message to use Joy to discern if you are on the right path. Check in with any given situation to see if it brings you Joy; if not you may be detouring from your path and it's time to course correct. With this advice, I have learned to navigate through the potholes, roadblocks and detours that come up on my journey through life. I came out of my dark, depressed, painful tunnel into the light of pure Joy.

It all began when a friend introduced me to the movie *The Secret*. I watched it and saw Jack Canfield speaking about headlights and that we don't have to see the whole road, we just need to see where the headlight shines and trust the rest of the road will appear. I felt something inside me hearing his words and I knew I wanted to learn more. I went to several seminars and learned valuable lessons such as taking 100% responsibility which empowered me to choose my healing path.

At first it was difficult to find and feel joy, but with persistence I found things that really made me happy. I started with small changes and equated this to calibrating my compass while I started crafting my new life. I made a list of things that made me happy, where I could feel a smile in my heart as this was my Joy Compass. It was simple, biking and BBQing made me smile, so I did more of those things. I found that the more joy-filled things I did the easier it became to recognize Joy. My Joy Compass was becoming a stronger more accurate guide.

With my compass in full effect now I started working on the deeper issues of healing and finding my soul's purpose and mission. I researched many healing modalities. There were several that worked and some that didn't resonate with me. I loved Jack Canfield's *The Success Principles* as it gave me a base to living life. Byron Katie's *The Work* helped me with healing emotional difficulties. Meditation and my gratitude journal became daily rituals. Later in the journey I super charged my process with *Aroma Freedom*.

As I gained strength and clarity, I delved into more ways of using my compass. I would ask myself, "How does this make me feel?" "Do I feel light and happy about this decision, or does it feel heavy?" "If I did this, how would it make me feel?" This allowed me to choose from a place of joy and happiness. One step led to another, more workshops, courses and events that were aligned with joy. Time passed and I found myself in a space of peace and calm and was ready to share with the world.

I have had the honor of helping numerous people find what brings them joy. One of the biggest honors was helping my parents on their path at their journey's end. One of my keys to healing was forgiveness.

We had beautiful talks in the months prior to their passing. I could truly see them through the eyes of compassion as they recounted their lives. I shared with them about my Joy Compass and the journey of my heart's purpose. They shared with me the many joys that life brought them, and times that were difficult to find joy in the event. Though our spiritual beliefs differed, toward the end of my mother's life we spent hours sharing our combined stories of life, love and joy. We cried, we laughed, and we loved. She had a strong faith in God that never wavered. We saw our commonalities in our beliefs; we just called them different things. As her final days on earth were approaching, she shared one last honor with me. She said that her Joy Compass was serving God. I could see her face light up with joy as she recounted the many stories and blessings that she had witnessed. When she passed, she had a radiant glow on her face, and I knew she was home.

It has been ten years since the day I discovered my Joy Compass. It has been an amazing winding road — a road I have been grateful to allow Joy to lead the way. Potholes of pain have led to a path of forgiveness and compassion. Detours of loss have placed me on the path of gratitude and love. A roadblock of cancer gave me my Joy Compass.

No matter where you are in your journey, I invite you to discover your Joy Compass because the world needs us to come alive. Navigate life with Joy and see what awaits. 🏵

Notes

Ilya Vita

❀

Ilya Vita is passionate about elevating, empowering, and enlightening women. She has been coaching and mentoring for over 15 years. With humor and care Ilya loves to assist people to find their authentic selves, define their definition of success, and guide them to that success.

She graduated from Jack Canfield's Train The Trainer program and received her certification in family, couple, and parent child coaching. Ilya is currently completing her training in RIM facilitator, NLP practitioner, and hypnotherapy practitioner, facilitator for an empowerment program for women in prison and halfway houses. Her global vision is women practicing cooperation, not competition for the betterment of the world.

Ilya is a transformational specialist. She is a trainer in personal and business achievement, not for profit business formation specialist, motivational speaker, coach in business, life and relationships. Ilya is blessed to have dog named Kitty that has demonstrated joy in the most trying of situations.

Contact
Website: www.labellavitaconsultants.com
Email: Ilya@LaBellaVitaConsultants.com

Rediscover Your Joyful Life

By Ilya Vita

"We need joy as we need air. We need love as we need water. We need each other as we need the earth we share."

— Maya Angelou

Many people in the world had an awakening when the pandemic hit in 2020. No longer were they rushing from one place to another. No longer could they escape the life they had created or had been created for them.

The isolation left us without outside support people. Those that we were left to isolate with caused us to examine our most intimate relationships. People tend to utilize others to give them a definition of self. You often adopt the ways of thinking and being, good or bad, of the people you spend the most time with. This is called the "Social Proximity Effect".

It seems more women than men have experienced this phenomenon, throughout history, even without a pandemic.

I remember a time in my life that I woke up and stumbled into the bathroom. I looked in the mirror and did not recognize the woman looking back at me. Where had that young woman gone? The woman who wanted to take on the world and be a writer. Since it was early morning, and these thoughts were too deep before I had coffee. I decided to take on my coffee pot instead of thoughts.

Imagine my surprise when I walked out of my bedroom and wondered who the hell had decorated my house?! The young woman I now was yearning to be never would have picked these colors and this style! As my children entered the kitchen I wondered where they came from, and I really was not sure I even liked them. They had attitudes. "Mom, why is my lunch not made? Mom, did you make the chili for today's chili cook off at school? Mom, why don't you know where my shoes are?"

I was shocked when a man walked into my kitchen pretending to be my husband! I know he was lying because the young woman I was when I went to sleep would have married someone completely different.

Was I having a breakdown? No, I was finally waking up to a life I had created. Just as the pandemic forced us to look at our lives.

How many times have you given up or given away your joy? I believe, like many great philosophers and poets, joy is our birthright. Babies live in joy. When they are out of joy, they will let you know it.

Before your head starts pounding from a headache trying to analyze all the ways throughout your life you gave away your joy, let's look at your day-to-day ways:

- Agreeing to do something that you do not want to do and being resentful of it
- Not sticking with your healthy boundaries
- Taking blame/responsibility for something you did not do
- Not being your authentic self
- Going along so you do not make waves
- Forgetting your essence
- Playing small so that others will be happy
- Not speaking up for your wants and needs
- Playing a role so that others will be comfortable
- Giving away your power
- Being a people pleaser
- Being a fixer
- Being in a codependent relationship
- Believing you are not enough
- Your internal dialog sounds like a 13-year-old mean girl

Do any of those things sound familiar?

Joy brings life to our external life, just as air brings life to our bodies. If we stop breathing, we die. If we stop having joy in our lives, it dies.

We wake up, just as I did in someone else's life. Someone who gave away their joy one small crumb at a time.

At the furniture store: Instead of buying the sofa that brought joy to her heart with the color and luscious fabric, she was talked into a color that would hide the dirt from her husband's Sunday football parties and a fabric that would wear longer.

The kids: Agreeing to participate in a chili cook off because she did not want to appear an absent parent. Despite the fact she was the sole bread winner of the family, had a job that was an hour commute, and had life or death responsibilities at work.

The Husband: Allowing his behavior in not participating in the responsibilities of raising children and laying on the ugly sofa she had come to resent.

For self: Not being authentic, instead of speaking up about the feelings she was having, eating them instead in an entire cheesecake, not investing in products that would make her feel better about herself, not prioritizing her health.

So, do you even know what brings you joy anymore? Have you lost yourself and do not even know what your favorite color is?

Here are a few suggestions:

- Join the app Meet Up. No, it is not a dating site. It is an app that you can look at groups that have varied interests near you. During COVID it was by Zoom, but now it is getting back to more normal. Explore old and new interests.

- Go to a park and sit under a tree. Brainstorm on a piece of paper the happiest time in your life. What was happening? Who was there? Then think of the second happiest time in your life and aske the same questions.

- After five memories start looking at the common factors. Was it because you were with friends? When was the last time you really spent time with friends being authentically you? Was it because you were in a learning environment? When was the last time you immersed yourself in learning something new?

- Grab a poster board and magazines that have different topics. Go through the magazines and start tearing out pictures that catch your interest. Start collaging. What is emerging on the board? Do you want to change your wardrobe and add more color? Do you want to travel more? Are you realizing you really do not like pastels in your home and want to dry more jewel tones?

After you have found the themes that bring you joy, make a plan to implement them into your life. It does not mean you have to plan that trip for an African Safari tomorrow, but you can start looking at the options on travel, read a book on African wildlife, start making a list of the items you will need to take with you, etc.

- What is something that someone does for you that makes you feel joy? Is it receiving flowers? A small gift? A thoughtful card?

Think of ways that you can do that for others. Giving to others and being of service not only brings joy to you but makes the world a much better place.

- What about the world, what can you do to contribute to society? It does not have to be as digging wells in a third world country. Although, if that is what brings you joy go for it!

I have a friend who goes to Costco and buys a case of water and a case of health bars each week. When she see's someone on a street corner she hands them a list of resources in the area that provide food, shelter, clothing, etc., a protein bar, and water. It brings her so much joy.

Another friend travels a lot for work, even during COVID. He collects all the travel size products from his hotel rooms and asks for extra from the hotel. Friends and family also collect for him. Once a month he takes the collection to a homeless shelter.

On Saturdays in the early morning hours, when most are sleeping, a group of volunteers descend on a beach near me. They walk the miles of beach picking up trash and debris. It prevents items from going into the water that could harm sea life and provides a beautiful clean beach for people to enjoy.

- When is the last time you bought yourself flowers, a candle, took a bubble bath, walked barefoot in the grass, put a wildflower in your hair, danced like a crazy person, sang out loud, walked on the beach and collected seashells, really listening to the birds singing or a bee buzzing?

- Write three things every day that you are grateful for. Close your eyes, think of each one individually, and really feel that feeling of gratitude.

"Research shows that daily experiences of awe, curiosity, gratitude, joy, and love can put the average person on a trajectory of growth, success, and positive social connection, and can also prevent those who are suffering from following a downward spiral."*

I believe one of the positive things that has come from the quarantine of 2020/2021 it is the fact that it forced us all to slow down and really look at ourselves, our lives, and the world as a whole.

The things we used to mask our lack of joy were for the most part stripped from us. It has become our responsibility to find our joy which will in turn make us better people not only for ourselves, those that we love and care about, as well as the world as a whole.

Joy is not only a birthright, but it is essential for our growth as individuals and for humanity. It was with us when we took our first breath and will be with us when we take our last.

I have been with many as they transitioned out of this world, and I have to say that all had joy as they did. Their bodies may have been in discomfort but in the end, they found joy in seeing Guardian Angels, departed loved ones, a beautiful location some called heaven, or an amazing light.

So put this book down, go experience joy, let it fill your heart and soul, and then share that joy with others.

When we have joy we have love not only for ourselves, for others, and the earth.

*Picture This! Bringing joy into Focus and Developing Healthy Habits of Mind: Rationale, design, and implementation of a randomized control trial for young adults (website: ncbi.nlm.nih.gov/pmc/articles/PMC6658827)

Jane Williams

❀

Jane Williams is an Intuitive Energy Coach & Performing Arts Educator who helps people break through blocks to help them be the most abundant and best version of themselves. As a graduate of Michigan State University, Virginia Tech and The Dell'Arte School of Physical Theatre, Jane has worked in the performing arts and creativity field all her life.

Jane is a Dow Creativity Fellow from Northwood University in Michigan and an Emerging Artist Recipient from the Durham Arts Council in North Carolina. She has completed Jack Canfield's & Kathleen Seeley's Train The Trainer Virtual Skills Bootcamp; is on her RIM journey with Dr. Deb Sandella & Michael Kline; is a Certified Barrett Values Centre Leadership & Coaching Consultant; and a CBR Certified Oracle Guide.

Jane is always looking for the best in people and how to unravel the "puzzle" of who they are and wish to become.

Contact

Website: www.janeawilliams.com
Email: jane@janeawilliams.com

A Woman of Simple Joys

By Jane Williams

"When despair for the world grows in me and I wake in the night at the least sound in fear of what my life and my children's lives may be, I go and lie down where the wood drake rests in his beauty on the water, and the great heron feeds. I come into the peace of wild things who do not tax their lives with forethought of grief. I come into the presence of still water. And I feel above me the day-blind stars waiting with their light. For a time I rest in the grace of the world, and am free."

— Wendell Berry

I consider myself a woman of simple joys.

Looking at my cat's face as he sleeps. I mean REALLY looking — at the pattern his fur swirls create; at his one white strand found in a myriad of midnight black; the concentration of his sleep on his closed eyelids; the way he is so relaxed and trusting in his home and my care. I fall in love with that face every time as his sleeping trust relaxes me. The expertise of how he stretches and flops with one single white paw curled up on his chest while the rest of his limbs and body take over a queen-sized bed. I envy his ability to expand to sizes five times his actual body and his mannerly acknowledgement that I am allowed the edge of the far side of that same bed.

I can watch the wind in the trees for hours — twisting and turning, rustling and resting, dancing and daring — in a conversation only the elements know. On days of unending heat and humidity found in summer months, I long and pray to see dancing leaves that "turn over to show their undersides." This farmer lore is from my Dad, a successful dairy farmer, who could always note when rain was coming because of this action from the trees. Now, every time I see this no matter where I am, I remember the sound of his voice and the calm certainty that this was so. I remember the feeling that this was good and needed in one's life, especially for the Earth, the soil that grows things, and for Mother Gaia.

I get lost in the bees who work my flowers. Their gentle bobbing from one blossom to the next, drinking their fill in their various black and golds. The large, colorful butterflies flitting throughout those same blossoms, dipping and sipping here and there. The lone Anna's Hummingbird who stands guard from other interlopers who dare enter the fragrant colorful world that is his, and only his.

I can stare at a spider building her intricate and delicate web. I marvel at the architecture passed on through her lineage. I feel the sorrow when I walk into that same web destroying all of her creation and can almost hear her sigh with a "let's begin again" whisper on the wind.

I have a large Barred Owl who lives outside my home. During the winter months, he perches solemnly and still. Just . . . waiting . . . watching . . . listening. He blends so well with the naked trees he is often invisible in full sight. I become enthralled and abandon everything else I am supposed to do in order to watch him out my window. I absorb his essence — his quiet confidence of stillness making him a sentinel in the woods. "Please make me as still and calm as you are in the midst of this world. Please. I need this so much right now."

We had a moment, he and I. I wanted to get closer; to really look at him. I went outside on my deck and sidled up behind a flower pole as quietly and softly as I could. He was fine. All of a sudden, he locked eyes on me. His eyes snapped yellow with narrow pupils as he lowered his head and danced at me. I lost my breath as he bobbed side to side and, being the courageous chicken that I am, without taking my eyes off his, I sidled back from whence I came. He was a continual visitor until workmen came to dig up behind my house. I didn't see him for a few months after that until just the other day. He came back to his perch and acknowledged me, camouflaged this time by the full summer leafing of the trees that are his home.

Water. I find joy in delicious streams of burbling, cool water that mesmerize me with their lullabies; that soothe me with their changing colors of little waves. Streams that sing to me of secrets to be explored. The larger shushing sounds of pounding ocean waves who start from far off lands and end their journeys on shores where I happen to be standing. The trickster waves of fun and delight from lakes; whitecaps from the power of the Great Lakes; the majesty of waterfalls; even water fountains in parks. Laughing, soothing, pulling me into daydreams and places of stillness and nothingness. Rainstorms — all rainstorms and their thunder and lightning, whether raucous or gentle. Storms that call my name every time and to whom I am happy to answer.

Snow. The hush of falling snow. The pristine beauty of this magical element that covers and reveals in its simplistic beauty. The deliciousness of being snowed in. The time when the world stops and is put on hold. The time when we can slow down, rest and breathe.

When I was younger, I would think of the word "JOY" in bright yellow and red colors — as firecrackers, confetti, stars and fireworks with crowds cheering. I would see cartoons exploding and jumping for the sheer excitement of joy! The frenetic feeling that we're supposed to feel with "JOY." "I've got that joy, joy, joy, joy down in my heart! WHERE? Down in my heart! WHERE? Down in my heart!" sung at full blast and a fast, fast, faster yet tempo. WHEEEEEEE!!!! Only to crash off the merry-go-round and bump my head, skin my knee, and scrape my hands trying to prevent the fall.

As an adult, there was a time in my life where I was pulled back into this frenetic pace again. Only this time it manifested itself in months of no sleeping or eating. Of unknown panic attacks that would freeze me in my tracks in the grocery store. Anxiety of things that never bothered me before. The back and forth, back and forth, back and forth of making decisions that were no big deal to others, but to me felt like my life would end if I didn't choose correctly. I have always viewed myself as a somewhat calm person — one who was very capable of making decisions — albeit a passionate, fiery and creative one. This frenetic feeling, this absolute feeling of being lost and not knowing where to turn, happened as a result of PTSD (post-traumatic stress disorder) diagnosed after my first school shooting. An event that happened very early in the never-ending string of school shootings in America.

And yes, my first, as I have now been through two.

This freneticism took over my life, only to have me crash from the sheer exhaustion of it all. As a kid, moments like this may just be all right as one could "shake it off." As an adult however, this freneticism continuing throughout daily life while assuring everyone around me that I was "fine, just fine," burned such a hole in my psyche that the resulting crash was a complete shut down. After months of supporting my colleagues while I myself wasn't eating or sleeping, I could no longer carry on. I moved from one state to another for a job to escape where I was at, only to move back again while never unpacking my moving van. I was told by people I trusted that all I "needed to do was work harder and longer." If I didn't do this I would end up "just like Aunt Elsie." I still don't understand that "threat" and really, was that so bad? I kind of like her. I was told constantly that it was because I "am an artist that's why I am like this!" Huh. And finally, "why don't I just get a gun and shoot myself" from a brother who said this not once but twice. After such supportive advice as this, I finally gave in. NONE of that was working. I stopped. I had to.

And, as a public high school choral and musical theatre director, this merry-go-round freneticism is the pace that I find is being demanded daily from educators all across the nation as we try to carry on for our students through a pandemic. I find this pace being demanded even WITHOUT the pandemic.

Nothing is enough. We as educators are not enough. We don't DO enough. We have to perform better, faster, farther, longer while doing all things for all students. We are mandated to be dieticians, social workers, psychologists, nurses, doctors, hand holders, safety experts, blue ribbon givers, keeping up scores from tests, mask puller-uppers, etc. ALL with NO concern for our own welfare. And especially our own joy. We are non-existent in the eyes of many even as we are their greatest resource.

With the help of the kindness of strangers, many friends and angels sent my way, I slowly but surely reclaimed myself. Not my old self, mind you, but a new and different version of myself. One I continue to redis-cover and greet anew each day. I find I often have to be more courageous than before as I "will" myself out and about, when I would prefer to stay out of the fray in my jammies with a good book. I seek out my friends so much more, as laughter brings the sunshine in and makes me feel connected. I sing more. And, I have compassion for others more.

But perhaps the most important path that has brought me to the truth of my new self is the presence of simple joys — of searching, seeking out and SAVORING the simple joys.

The joy of the crunch of snow under my walking feet as my Dad and I head back to the house after milking his dairy herd. The joy of listening to the purr of my boy Louie who so often pulls me out of myself. The joy of looking up at the stars and planets in the clear night sky. The absolute joy, laughter, silliness and camaraderie of friends who know and under-stand me, but more importantly, ACCEPT me, brokenness and all.

And the joys of being a woman OF simple joys that lull me into my new self — a more authentic self — time and time again like the pound-ing ocean waves from far-off lands reaching a shore where I happen to be standing, ready to begin again. 🏵

Su Stacey

❀

Su Stacey is a 64 year young mother, grandmother, friend and novice writer. She lives in Silver Lake, NH at The Ripple. Su is a bookkeeper by trade with over 35 years of experience, but her career is motherhood.

She loves to cook and entertain, creating joy with those she nourishes. Su mostly loves spending time with her grandchildren as they fill her heart with joy. She loves to share her wisdom with them and experience each of their unique personalities.

Su is certified in Reiki and practices spiritual growth, learning as much for herself and to help others. She is certified in hypnosis and RIM Essentials, through Dr. Deb Sandella. She attended Break Through to Success and is certified in Train the Trainer with Jack Canfield. Su finds joy in exploring alternative healing methods; learning the attributes of precious gemstones, essential oils, mediumship and other forms of the metaphysical realm.

Contact

Personal Website: www.sustacey.com (in development)
Business Website: www.abcswithsu.com

The Joy of Becoming a Grandmother

By Su Stacey

"Being a mother and grandmother is the best of the best in my life. My grandchildren multiply the joy my daughters bring me."

— Alexandra Stoddard

I dropped everything, grabbed my packed bag and drove two hours to be at the hospital where my oldest daughter, Barbs, was planning to give birth to my first grandchild! When I arrived, I offered to be with Barbs if Brian wanted to get some fresh air and something to eat.

I sat by her head, gently running my fingers thru her hair, like I used to do when she was young. I remembered when she was three and wanted me to fix it with a bow to match her outfit. At seven she insisted on a side braid, like the girl in a magazine and when she was sixteen readying for her prom she asked me to be sure the back of her hair was in place. On her wedding day, she asked me to carefully place the veil on her head. Recalling all those moments brought tears of joy to my eyes, as I knew she was about to embark on another episode, motherhood, that would change her life forever.

Barbs was so brave as her labor was not progressing.

The consulting doctor introduced himself and told Barbs and Brian he needed to perform a C-section, as they were concerned with the baby's fluctuating heart rate. A look of alarm crossed both their faces, as Barbs nodded her head in acceptance. I saw my daughter go from wanting medication for her pain to understanding the need to have her baby be born safely. She put her child's needs first, deciding what was best for the baby. Watching this compassionate act, I saw my daughter, become a mother. The joy of witnessing my child become a mom was indescribable.

My grandson Tanner James, who I lovingly call Teej, was born, healthy, fully awake and perfect in every way!

I stayed at their house for a week once Barbs and Tanner arrived home. Each morning around five, Barbs would bring Tanner to me all fed and wide awake, while she went back to bed to get a few solid hours of sleep. I'd burp and change him, then I'd prop him up on my knees as I sat against the wall in my bed so I could look at him and coo as I told him stories. I cherished these moments and can still remember the fullness in my heart from those mornings. I cried most of my way home. I was torn, wanting to stay, yet knowing I had to get back to my life two hours away.

My truth is I don't think of motherhood as a sacrifice but rather a part of who I am. I simply do whatever it takes to keep my children and grandchildren feeling loved, safe and healthy. I can't imagine my life without caring for them. I'm happiest when their arms are around my neck or my phone buzzes with a text from the older ones or I snap a photo of family spending time together. Pure joy.

I love my visits with Tanner, whenever we can be together, playing, chatting or exploring. When he was nine months old I had gotten him a toy cell phone which I was able to record a message. I recorded, "Always remember Grammi loves her Teej!" To this day I send him texts and leave him voice mail messages with that phrase. I know he secretly loves it.

The summer Tanner turned six, he became a big brother. My grandson Liam was born in August that year. I stayed for a week helping Barbs, taking Tanner to football practices, helping with household chores and of course early morning baby cuddles with Liam. Driving Tanner provided us quality Grammi time to talk about Tanner's world.

Last spring was Tanner's golden birthday, he turned seventeen on May 17th. Even though it was during the early months of the pandemic, I made him his favorite dessert "Uncle Ian's birthday hamburger cookies" and my famous ice cream cake. I drove two hours to surprise him.

Tanner suggested we go on a hike. He drove Liam and I followed in my car. Going for hikes in his area had become our routine adventure. He always brought me to a new place with an easy walk, unlike the mountain hikes I used to take him on when he would visit me. I wasn't in as good of shape as I was back then.

It was a beautiful spring morning walking through a field, into the woods, and finally we came out to the ocean. The scene took my breath away. Tanner said, "See Grammi I told you it was a good one." Looking at him and his brother from behind as they took in the view made my heart swell. I joyfully thought how many seventeen and eleven-year-old boys would want to spend time hiking with their grandmother and be appreciative of such a lovely place.

Reflecting on my own teen years, they were very different than Tanner's. When I was sixteen, I had a baby girl I gave up for adoption. I wanted to give her the best opportunity in life. I had a lot of fear and confusion around the decision. Some may call it sacrifice. For me it was and still is a most profound act of courageous love. We were reunited when she was nineteen, which, by far, was the most surreal day of my life. Her name is Robyn. I'm known as her birth mom and respectively honor her adoptive mother as her mom. I remember when Robyn called to tell me her daughter, Courtney, had arrived and invited me to visit them. I was so happy for Robyn and so excited to meet my granddaughter. I remember Robyn lovingly gazing at her daughter as I held her in my arms. She asked, "How hard was it for you to give me up?" I took a deep breath, then said, "I knew I wasn't old enough to raise a child, as I was just a child myself. I may have put you up for adoption, but I never gave you away. You have always been in my heart."

To this day I'm Grammi Su to her children. I loved welcoming her and her children into my family and seeing how love and joy shines through all of us if we show up with an open heart.

I suppose I can best sum it all up rather simply. Sacrifice, devotion, courage all boils down to love and joy if we let it.

When Courtney was three her twin brothers were born, Trevor and Brayden. I visited the weekend before the boys arrived. Courtney and I played Cinderella, she twirled in her sparkling flowy dress and of course she wore a tiara! I loved her delightful giggle, as I would bow as the prince and ask her to dance.

My visits with them are infrequent, however we pack a lot of fun and quality time into them. I enjoy stepping into Robyn's world and sharing time with her and her children. Robyn's mom and I, both pour our love into our grandchildren.

After being a grandmother for ten years, Nikki, my youngest daughter, wrote me poem telling me she was going to have a baby. As soon as I realized what the poem meant, I felt a tingle in my heart. I knew instantly the baby was going to be a girl! She was due the end of March according to the mid-wife. Nikki and Kyle chose a different birth experience outside of the hospital at a place called the Birth House. The house was an old Victorian style home where there was a school for midwives in the front area and the birthing room in the back.

One snowy February morning, Kyle called to say Nikki wanted me to come to their house. He believed Nikki was in labor. I said, "No, it's too early, she still has another month to go." I was thinking, 'It's just Braxton-hicks contractions'.

Once I got there I agreed today would likely be the day, as I discovered Nikki's water had broken earlier that morning. They left to drive the 35 minutes to the Birth House. I drove their dog to my house and would meet them there. Oh, did I mention it was a blizzard that day . . . anyone who knows me, knows I do not drive in that stuff, however today was different my granddaughter was arriving!

Nikki and Kyle had not wanted to know the baby's gender and had two names picked out. Violet for a girl. I don't recall the boy's name, to me it did not matter, I knew the baby was a girl! Nikki was in the huge birthing tub with Kyle kneeling at the side rubbing her back. There were three midwives surrounding the other side of the tub. I couldn't see much but on occasion I would climb up the steps to the tub to peek over and touch Nik on the head to let her know I was there to give her mom's support.

Then it happened. I saw it! A little head popped out and then her shoulders. The midwife told Nik she could reach down and gently pull her baby out. She put her hands around the tiny shoulders and gently guiding her baby out and onto her chest. "It's a girl!" the midwife said. I stepped back to let them do their work. The baby was so quiet and the midwife instructed Nikki and Kyle to talk to their daughter to welcome her. The midwife closest to the baby rubbed her back. I could only see a little purple foot that I took a picture of with my phone. We had not had time to discuss if photos were allowed.

The room was silent, then there was a gasp as the baby opened her eyes and ever so lightly let out a small soft cry. Tears poured down my cheeks. I was filled with such joy. She was alive, a girl, small yet healthy! Again I was blessed to witness my baby girl turn from daughter to mother! My granddaughter Violet Marie was born, tiny, adorable and healthy; filling us all with love! I visited them every day after work, helping Nikki and getting cuddle time with Violet.

Violet became a big sister three times over the next five years and they all call me Mimi. I am fortunate to see my younger four grandchildren regularly, as they live only half an hour away on a farm. I fondly refer to them as my farm girls. One favorite activity at Mimi's is tub time, they love to play with the bath toys that were their mom's.

Violet and her sisters are delightful, creative, challenging and loving. Their giggling squeals of happiness over chasing bubbles is so infectious, that I've recorded them. On days I'm not able to be with them, I watch the video and the spark of joy ignites.

Joy may be a three letter word, so small yet so powerful it holds such an amazing perception for the tingly feelings swirling around ones being when they experience it. When a spark of joy seeps in, a smile starts that travels down filling my heart, tickling my belly and then like a flash my brain is illuminated as my being becomes lighter.

I have been blessed with nine grandchildren; Tanner, Courtney, Trevor, Brayden, Liam, Violet, Maggie, Ellie and Caroline. My favorite times are spent with them. They energize and exhaust me and fill me with such love and joy. I love being a grandmother, being able to hug and provide special attention to each child. I believe it is important that each one knows they are loved, unique individuals who are a special gift to this world.

The challenges I've had in life are the very things that have helped me develop courage and fully experience love and joy. I have the honor of watching my daughters do the same with my grandchildren.

I may do bookkeeping as a 'job' but my 'career' is being a mother and grandmother. ✤

Notes

Diane Palmer

———— ✿ ————

Diane was born in Detroit, Michigan as a second generation Italian-American; the third daughter of four. After many years of emotional and physical abuse handed out by her father, her mom decided to get a divorce and they moved away.

She got married in 1982 and after two years of being physically, emotionally, and verbally abused by her husband, she left. Diane refused to raise her children in the same environment that she had been raised in as a child.

Eventually this took her to the greater Seattle area. She was now finally on the path to becoming her true self. In finding her strength and stepping into her power, she also found the love of her life, Bob Palmer . . . Her greatest love.

She is now a successful investor as well as a co-author of an Amazon #1 Best Seller. She also assists Bob at their workshops, where they help others find their path to success through Palmer motivation.

Contact
Website: www.palmermotivation.com

Happiness vs. Joy

By Diane Palmer

"Joy is a beautiful sunrise, the giggle of a grandchild, and knowing you're truly loved. It's the little things in life that make up our joyful moments. Joy, like a good glass of wine, comes in sips, not gulps."

— Diane Palmer

My love (Bob) and I, enjoy being up early when we're on vacation and watching the sun rise over the ocean waves. Spending time together is one of life's pleasures that means so much to both of us. We also love being with our grandchildren and hearing them giggle without worry of how they sound. Those giggles make me smile for hours, long after the moment has passed. It's a beautiful time in their lives when they haven't learned to be self-conscious. They're not worried what other people think. They're enjoying their play.

I love that the joys of life are all around us. They come in an instant and sometimes are gone in a second, yet they touch my soul. They stir me deep inside. My hope is that I continue to learn to appreciate and savor them to their fullest, because joy, like a good glass of wine, comes in sips, not gulps.

Many folks toss around the words happy and joy without thinking much about them. For me, there is a big difference between these two words.

My Love and husband, Bob, and I put on workshops and do trainings to help people get in touch with who they are deep down. We help them realize their life purpose and who they want to be and how they want to show up in the world on a daily basis. We do this work because we discovered things about ourselves as we were going through similar workshops, and the impact of this work on our lives was profound. So, we decided to take on the challenge of teaching and sharing these concepts in order that others would learn and grow in their lives and reach more joyous levels of happiness.

Looking at the difference between happiness and joy is relatively simple.

Happiness lives on the surface. It keeps us going and makes all those tiny moments matter. Happiness puts a smile on our face and a lift in our step. But in an instant, our smile can turn to disappointment and even rage if the situation turns a different way. My example is seen at Disneyland, known as "The Happiest Place On Earth." We hear kids crying and parents scolding. If this is the happiest place, then why all the tears?

Joy, on the other hand, is something that lives deep down inside of us. It's in our soul. It's in our being. We can have joy or be filled with joy, and still have some sadness, because joy runs deeper than happiness or sadness. Happiness and sadness have the ability to come and go, while joy is more steady. More even. Our joy is what keeps us engaging in life, despite our sadness or set backs.

Our joy is what sustains us despite our disappointments in people or situations. Our joy keeps us moving forward and striving to get better and do better.

I was first introduced to the notion of joy through training events my husband and I did with Jack Canfield several years ago. Until then, I had never given the difference between happiness and joy much thought. As soon as we started learning about our purpose in life, and the things that drove us, that is when the notion of real joy and true happiness started to settle within me. I started to realize that making joy happen and capitalizing on that joy as we went forward was something that was very important to me.

I suggested my idea to Bob of something I wanted to call our 'Joy Box'. I wanted to have something that we could use to capture our special moments as we went through the year. This would be something that we could add to as the year went by. It could be anything. A note from a friend, tickets to a movie, date night, an evening out, a pedal from a bouquet of flowers given to me. Anything at all. Anything that had brought me or us joy during the year. There were no limits on what it could be, but I wanted something that we could use to go back and treasure times throughout the year that had brought us joy and special meaning.

We decided to set aside an honored time to go through our 'Joy Box' and relive the moments that made our year so great. We decided that the best time to do this would be on New Year's Eve. With snacks and a bottle of wine, we would light a fire and sit on the floor and open the 'Joy Box' and go through the contents of the past year remembering all those moments that brought us so much Joy. Bob and I take turns reaching into the box and pulling out whenever is next or whatever we find to grab. We read whatever it is. Each item we capture is followed by laughter and smiles and recalling fond memories.

The first time we did this, it was apparent how many moments we had already forgotten, even though they had only happened a few months back. The memories brought smiles as well as joyful tears as we walked our way through the past year.

This one simple idea that I had has brought us more joy than you can imagine. We look forward to New Year's Eve more now than ever because of this simple, meaningful idea.

A second thought around celebrating joy is something that happened more organically than planned. Bob taught high school for several years and received encouraging notes on occasion from students, parents, faculty and administrators. Without much thought as to what it might be, he decided one day to pin these notes to a blank spot on the wall in his classroom. In a surprisingly short time, the space on the wall started filling up with notes and cards overflowing with encouragement. The students started noticing the section on the wall growing as well. It turned into Bob's version of his 'Joy Box.'

If he ever felt like he wasn't making a difference or that things weren't going as well as he had hoped, he found himself looking to the left of his desk and seeing a full wall of encouragement. When students, teachers and administrators would visit his classroom they noticed his spot on the wall. They would ask what it was? Bob would tell them it was his 'Joy Wall.' In the four short years that Bob created his 'Joy Wall' it filled a solid space 5 feet by 5 feet in his classroom.

These simple ideas have brought us more joy than you can imagine. The 'Joy Box' has become our favorite relationship tradition and there is always a wall that needs decorating with encouragement.

I would recommend that everyone engage in the 'Joy Box' for a year and see how they could create a 'Joy Wall' somewhere in their life. See what you think. My guess is you will learn to love and embrace this as much as we have.

I hope these two simple ideas will serve as encouragement for you to look for and embrace the Joy in your own lives that might be slipping away without being noticed. It's through these simple things that we have come to realize it really is the little things that bring us true and lasting joy. And learning how to save and remember these moments has made all the difference in our lives.

So many of us never think to make an investment in ourselves or take the time for self-care.

One thing that I've learned in my own personal development and growth is, that your mess is your message. And if you can help just one person by sharing your message, your mess was worth sharing.

You can't change the world for everybody, but you can change it for somebody. ⚘

Notes

Ann Smith Gordon

---❀---

Ann is a gifted writer and photographer who is descended from one of the founding settlers of Bermuda in 1616 and still resides there today.

Ann's life of service began as a child as she took care of her dolls, friends, cousins and anyone who would submit to the "treatment." She graduated as a Registered Nurse in 1956.

She has served Bermuda as a tourist guide, lobster fisherwoman, business owner and President and CEO of P.A.L.S. (Cancer Care in Bermuda) for 33 years retiring at age 80.

Ann has received countless awards: Most prestigious is becoming an MBE (Member of the Most Excellent Order of the British Empire) "For Services to the Community of Bermuda" by Queen Elizabeth II at Buckingham Palace on 22 October 1996.

Ann resides at her charming waterfront home where her prolific and historical writing continues daily laced with her generous dose of talented wit and incredible memory of adventures of her life on the treasured isle of Bermuda.

Journeys of Joy

By Ann Smith Gordon, R.N. MBE, JP

*"Though we travel the world over to find the beautiful,
we must carry it with us or we find it not."*

— Ralph Waldo Emerson

Perhaps it is because most of my childhood was spent in hospitals being prodded and jabbed and then in 1943, during World War II, hearing doctors telling my Mother and Dad that if they did not take me away to America for diagnosis and treatment, then I would surely die.

That was not joyful news but after two years of injections and doctors and pokes and jabs and a very strict diet of only 5 foods it was a joy indeed to return to my beloved Bermuda Island home. At last, I could enjoy what most children take for granted: ice cream, birthday cake, turkey at Christmas and sweets and treats all denied to me for what seemed like forever. But it did instill in me a strict sense of discipline, which I must admit 75 years later, has now faltered.

But all along the way have been memorable experiences of love and laughter, of sadness and hope, a sense of accomplishment and some 30 years of wonderful travel experiences all recorded as documentaries and presented annually to benefit the cancer care charity, PALS which I headed for 33 years, stepping down on my 80th birthday in 2015.

The joy of travelling for me began in 1958. I had been married in May of that year and worked long and hard for the next five months to save enough money to embark on what became a six- month journey in Europe. I travelled not with the bridegroom but with two school friends Jean Moss and Ann Harnett whose father kindly shipped his 10 year old Morris Minor to London for us to drive around Europe in style. We survived the trip but after 10,000 miles the poor car did not and died of exhaustion!

The idea was to follow my bridegroom who, by now was a Lt [junior grade] officer in the United States Navy serving as signalman and communications officer on board the massive aircraft carrier, USS Randolph, now on a Mediterranean cruise.

We were sitting on benches in Cannes on the Promenade de la Croisette, the beautiful waterfront avenue lined with cafes, luxury hotels, boutiques and restaurants when over the horizon loomed the huge Randolph. It was a moment in time I shall never forget.

But another thrill of a lifetime for us still lay ahead. At the time, October 1958, Sir Winston Churchill was staying with friends in a villa not far away. He accepted an invitation from the Captain of the Randolph to visit the ship but only on the strict condition that there would be no advance publicity, no reporters and no cameras. Amazingly our little trio was invited to be aboard to witness this historic event, marking Sir Winston's first visit to a US warship since World War II.

We accepted the invitation without hesitation and were taken out to the Randolph lying at anchor off shore by one of the ship's launches and escorted to a perfect viewing perch just above the assembled officers and crew all standing tall and strong in formation. It was indeed an impressive sight. Before long the helicopter carrying the guest of honour appeared out of the clear, blue sky and landed on the Randolph's deck only a few yards below us.

Using the words written by the bridegroom, 'The USS Randolph rendered him full honours and ceremonies.' It was indeed a most touching sight for us all 'to witness the grand old man of age 84 and frail from the burdens of war climb without help from the helicopter and proceed to inspect the marine honour guard as they had probably never been inspected before.' How proud we were to share this special moment in the presence of a truly great man whose spirit and fortitude carried the free world through the horrors of a second world war. I shall never forget that day.

One of the best parts of travel for me has always been the planning, the research and anticipation. But there can always be surprises such as the thrilling afternoon on the Randolph.

We were so lucky on this journey around Europe to find a parking place directly in front of our hotel every night. I use the word 'hotel' loosely. Our nightly lodging would not be considered five star but it was certainly adequate and it only cost us the equivalent of $3.00 each a night as we shared one room with a double bed and a single bed and the bathroom somewhere down the hall. For the first couple of weeks we flipped a coin for the single bed and I always won but soon my companions cried foul and from then on we took turns in strict rotation. On one occasion we arrived quite late in a town and were grateful to find lodging only to discover too late that it was a brothel and there was no key to the door! We piled all the furniture against the door and managed to get a few hours sleep in spite of the goings on below!

Everywhere we went we made friends. In Vienna the night watchman liked us so much that on his day off he insisted on spending the day with us showing off his beloved city and the Vienna Woods. It was more unexpected joy for us.

Imagine 1958 and three young Bermudians who had never explored the wonderful world of classical music and ballet. Our first ballet experience was in Vienna at the beautiful Vienna Opera House with the famous Kirov Ballet dancing Swan Lake. It was pure magic and a memory I have carried with me all these years. Another such memory never erased from my mind was in Milan when we somehow got tickets for the beloved opera La Boheme at the very famous La Scala Opera House where we were enthralled by the glorious production. Both these experiences led to a lifelong love of opera and ballet enjoyed in the famous great theatres of Europe.

For me travel has always been a learning experience. It is not always beautiful, not always comfortable and not always convenient. It can sometimes be sad even tragic but it can also be joyful. On both my journeys to Egypt I experienced many of these emotions. There are enchanting and magical countries whose very names reach toward a dream world beyond the setting sun. Egypt is such a country with many joys for me beginning in Cairo. We arrived very late on a dark night and went directly to the hotel, exhausted of course.

It was dawn when I awoke eager to have a first look at this ancient land. Our hotel, the famous Mena House is situated just below the timeless Pyramids and when I thrust the curtains back, there before my eyes was the first sight of the three Pyramids of Giza which have dominated the landscape for thousands of years. Times such as this have become engraved in the mind.

One such memory includes riding a beautiful Arabian horse at the Pyramids. The owner said not to let him "full out" as I would never stop him. So there I was alone on this highly spirited animal galloping at what seemed like breakneck speed through the sand past the Great Pyramid and toward the horizon. I can still feel the wind in my face.

I had another ride in Egypt. This time it was on a galloping camel. I was the only one of our small group who accepted the invitation instead of a long, hot trudge through the sand to reach a remote tomb. His name was Whisky and Soda, which may explain his enthusiasm. I hung on for dear life but did manage a proper Royal wave as we hurtled past my exhausted friends!

A heart-warming incident occurred at a small village along the River Nile. Of all the barefoot village children who crowded around us, there was another barefoot child in a green dress with a lovely face and a very sore bleeding toe covered in dirt. By sign language, I managed to make her understand that I would give her enough money to buy a pair of shoes. This I did. As our riverboat pulled away from the rough dock amid the shouting and chaos of the other children, there she stood, alone and away from the other children, waving quietly with the most wonderful expression of unspoken gratitude. Today, 40 years later, I can still vividly see that lovely little face so full of gratitude.

Another memory of joy in Egypt took place at the Nobles Tombs in the Valley of the Kings when a child came up to me and by sign language invited me into her home, an invitation I could not refuse.

In a dark kitchen I found the Mother cooking over an open fire and three little boys dressed only in little shirts playing on the dirt floor.

Again by sign language I was given permission to take their picture and then the question of how I could send them copies of the photos as no one could write their names or address. So, my little friend took charge again and raced away returning with a scribe. This was the beginning of a wonderful relationship by correspondence with Zanab. She was always able to find a scribe to write to me. I sent them parcels of clothes purchased from our Salvation Army store including a pair of shoes for Zanab whose size was determined by a piece of string she sent me.

Due to a travel agent mistake, we had a chance to return to Egypt the following year so there were many more visits to the Salvation Army and Margaret Tricker, my dear friend and companion, and I departed Bermuda armed with a huge duffle bag stuffed with clothes, shoes, treats and even tennis balls.

What a wonderful morning we had at Zanab's home, a big house without a roof and an unexplored tomb within the walls. It literally took hours to unpack the duffle bag with all the family present. As each garment came out one at a time there were shrieks of delight in deciding who should receive it. There were more than enough for everyone, the Mum, Hannam; the Dad Ibrahim; Zanab and the wee boys.

To repay us, the family insisted that we return the next morning at 10am for lunch. An invitation we were determined to accept even risking the dreaded "Delhi belly". They wanted to give us the very best and Hannam was up at dawn to prepare the feast. No doubt, it was a feast they could not afford. We sat on a rough wooden bench and the pigeon was served on chipped enamel bowls. The children sat on the dirt floor watching us. Of course there were no utensils to eat with and later the children drank from the by now disgusting "finger bowls."

When it was time to leave and we saw the family for the last time, all the Bermuda clothes had been washed and hanging on the line to dry. They all cried and when I asked Ibrahim what I could send him from Bermuda, his answer astonished me. I had expected a wish for a radio or batteries or something expensive but he replied: "A letter from you is a present for me". This from a man most tourists would consider a nuisance by pestering them to buy his trinkets yet his request to me was so humble. What joy those two days were for me. I can still see the family wiping the tears from their eyes as we drove away. For years I received letters from Zanab written by various scribes often beginning with words such as 'my dear sweet sister Ann.'

And so we also bid a sad farewell to this ancient land at the dawning of yet another day. The enchantment of Egypt with its proud, charming and hospitable people will remain a joy forever. ✸

Notes

JAN FRASER INSPIRED LIFE SERIES

Sharing

JOY

❀ ❀ ❀ ❀ ❀

Trisha Jacobson

Trisha Jacobson is passionately committed to helping people breakthrough fear, overcome blocks and heed the intuitive whispers and heart's wisdom along the path to self-discovery. She is an intuitive and compassionate teacher, a certified success principles trainer and best selling author who engages her readers, audiences and coaching clients; teaching conscious, subconscious and heart-centered tools to raise confidence, connect with purpose and create results that lead to more joy, happiness, success and fulfillment. She is also the founder and owner of Ripple on Silver Lake, a wonderful, heart centered retreat center nestled in the beautiful lakes region and White Mountains of New Hampshire.

Contact

Websites: www.trishajacobson.com and
www.rippleonsilverlake.com

Messages from a Manatee

By Trisha Jacobson

"Life is difficult. This is a great truth, one of the greatest truths. It is a great truth because once we truly see this truth, we transcend it. Once we truly know that life is difficult, once it is accepted, the fact that life is difficult no longer matters."

— M. Scott Peck, *The Road Less Traveled*

So what if it's all perfect just the way it is? What if the best thing we can do in our busy, often challenging, lives is to slow down our breathing, focus on gratitude, and expand joy as we take our next step?

On August 20, 1996, I sat on a bench in DeSoto Park in Bradenton, Florida with my Aunt Barbara. What would have been my eighth wedding anniversary instead had become the final stage of my divorce. I was so grateful for her invitation to get away from it all, the support she gave me through the process, and for this beautiful spot. As we sat on the bench overlooking the river, we talked about the challenges I had faced through my husband's addiction and the grief and sadness I was feeling as I fully accepted that my marriage was over.

Suddenly we heard a huge splash as a manatee jumped out of the water. He swam and romped and played in front of us for several min-utes, almost as if to invite us to put away the sadness for just a few minutes and join him for a dose of pure Joy. We both delighted in the show and then sat quietly for a while longer as we watched the sunset.

That day I learned some things: there is something about observing nature that grounds me and connects me to the power of gratitude; there is something about being in the present moment with gratitude that seems to open the door to Joy, that it is actually possible to feel gratitude in the very same moment I'm feeling sad, and that I can experience joy in the midst of great pain and grief. I also learned that Joy shared with another somehow compounds the experience and that laughing out loud enhances it even further.

I can still remember the exact moment my Mom told me she had made the decision to die. Her health struggles began a couple of years before with a fall that took her off the golf course and into intensive physical and occupational therapy for an injured hip. She fought hard, followed her treatment plan and ultimately reached her goal to get back on the golf course. She was proud of her accomplishment and so happy to be back out there.

A few months later she suffered a stroke that started the whole process all over again. My parents were living in a retirement community in Florida and were surrounded by an amazing support system; however, Mom's health condition required additional resources as her health declined. I became her healthcare proxy, and my life quickly became a series of last-minute scheduling changes based on what was happening with Mom.

If you've ever been the primary caretaker of an aging parent, you know what I was experiencing; overwhelming stress, frustration, and immense sadness watching my mother decline as, little by little, she began losing her quality of life. She was depressed and frustrated, but she was motivated and determined to get back on the golf course once again, and I was committed to doing everything I could to help her get there.

I was in California in the middle of running a live training event for one of my clients. I got a text from my brother Kevin that said, "Call me when you have some time to talk." My brother rarely called to just talk. I immediately sensed that something was wrong. I called him on our lunch break. He asked me to sit down and just listen. I heard him tell me about his persistent headaches, a myriad of test results, an oncology referral, metastases and cancer staging. "With your healthcare background in oncology, I know you know the odds aren't good, but it's important to me that I fight them. It's also important to me that you're there when I tell Mom about my diagnosis. Will you please do that for me? Will you fly to Florida over the next week or so and be there when I tell her?"

His news took my breath away. He was my younger brother. He had a successful career, a beautiful home, a wife, two teenagers and terminal brain cancer. As soon as we hung up, I rerouted my return flight home to New Hampshire, and a few days later, I flew into the Sarasota-Bradenton airport. I traveled a lot, and Mom and Dad were always happy to see me for my surprise visits, so it was as if nothing was wrong. We enjoyed a lovely dinner together. We looked at some family pictures Mom had found, and she was excited as she told me about her progress in physical therapy. She had Hope again, and I was grateful to share it with her, knowing that the next day, her hope would most likely be shattered.

The next day I watched her bright blue eyes go from dancing and happy, hearing Kevin's voice on the phone, to glazed and solemn as he shared his news. She stayed strong for him, but she hung up the phone and sat on the couch and simply stared at his picture hanging on the den wall. She had no words. She had no tears. She was in shock. After a while she announced that she was going to lie down. An hour later I went in to check on her.

She was lying across her bed, surrounded by crumpled up tissues with tears streaming down her face. I lay quietly with her for what seemed like forever. She finally spoke, "I don't think he's going to make it through this. I need to be on the Other Side for him. I'm ready to leave this life."

I remember being shocked at her words, but I also remember promising to support her, whatever she decided. A few days later Mom stopped all treatments. Eventually she stopped eating. Ultimately, she was admitted to hospice. She was at peace with her decision to die and, as difficult as it was, I was at peace with my decision to support her. I will always be grateful for the time she and I spent together and for lots of joyful moments we shared as she neared the end. At some point in the midst of it all, I made a decision that no matter what was happening around me, I needed to do three things:

1. Take time each day to spend some time focusing only on my breath.
2. Take time each day to reflect on what I am grateful for.
3. Do something intentionally each day that brings me Joy.

Before these practices became a habit, I had to set an alarm on my phone with reminders:

1. Take three deep breaths now!
2. Make a list of five things you are grateful for in this moment!
3. Look for Joy NOW!
4. It's time to go find the sunset!

Despite all the challenges, I began to notice that my conversations with my Mom, my family members, healthcare providers and strangers were more present and connected. I enjoyed daily sunsets at beach. I noticed families walking together, children playing, birds dancing along the shore and the feeling of the breeze on my face as the sun put on its spectacular show. Sometimes I expanded that joy by stopping for ice cream on the way back to face whatever was happening.

September 27, 2017 was no different. I spent the day at Mom's bed-side. She was non-responsive but, according to the nurses, still holding on and not showing any signs of transitioning. I was exhausted. As much as I wanted my Mom to hold on, I was finally ready for her to let go. My alarm went off to remind me that it was time to head to the beach to watch the sunset. I welcomed the break from the daily bedside ritual.

I always went to the beach, but that evening I automatically headed to DeSoto Park. I hadn't been there in years. As I parked the car and walked to the water, I felt drawn to the very same bench I had sat on with my Aunt Barbara over twenty years before. She had long since passed. My Mom needed her help. I sat on the bench and talked to her. I asked her to come help her sister. I asked her to guide my Mom through a peaceful transition, with grace and ease and without fear.

Tears streamed down my face as I reflected on the finality of losing my Mom. Suddenly I felt an immense sense of peace come over me. In that instant, a manatee popped out of the water right in front of where I was sitting. I got goose bumps all over my body. I laughed out loud as the manatee put on the same show it had put on for me and my Aunt over twenty years before. The sun began to set. I can still remember the gratitude and joy I felt in that moment at the very same time I was feeling sadness over the imminent loss of my Mom.

A few moments later, I felt a sudden urge to return to the Hospice House. Her nurse met me at the door and told me that Mom had begun her transition. I called Dad and my brother Keith. We all witnessed Mom take her last breath. We watched in amazement as a soft, peaceful look came over her face as her spirit left her body and moved into the corner of the room where she had often told me the spirits were waiting for her. I'm sure Aunt Barbara was there.

My heart broke with the reality of losing my Mom, but at the same time, I felt incredible joy for bearing witness to the entire experience and for fully understanding of the power of a mother's love for her children. I'm sure Mom was there to meet Kevin when he passed six months later.

I still practice deep breathing, Gratitude and Joy, in my daily life. I still experience challenges, sadness, grief and fear. We all do. However, I've discovered what I have come to know, that these practices help me stay connected to Joy, no matter what. I've learned that sadness, grief and fear can coexist with gratitude, love and joy. We can experience each of them separately, all of them together, or we can choose which one we'd like to focus on in any given moment. We get to choose!

I invite you to consider that the key to fully enjoying the magic life has to offer lies in living in gratitude, love and joy. I've found that these questions help me get there, especially during life's challenges. I hope they help you too.

- What if it's all perfect just the way it is?
- What if the challenges we face in life are simply to serve our learning, growing and becoming our best selves?
- What if, in times of difficulty, the only question we ask is, "What opportunity is there in this experience for me to learn and grow?"
- What if the only thing we do is focus on becoming fully present wherever we are while focusing on just one thing we are grateful for in that moment?
- What if we kept a list of some simple things that bring us joy and intentionally decide to do one of those things to intentionally raise our vibration in the moment?
- What if we strive to approach each and every day like Winnie the Pooh does?

"What day is it?" Pooh asked.
Piglet answered, "It's today."
Pooh said, "My favorite day!" 🏵

Notes

Lila Larson

───── ❀ ─────

L ila Larson is an international author, speaker, coach, mentor, consultant and trainer with experience in the Corporate, Private, Government, Education, Informational Technology, and Non-profit sectors. Her experience as a leader both locally and nationally has resulted in bottom line results for her clients. Her current book soon to be released follows Lila Larson's Leadership Philosophy: Clarity, Focus, Results.

Her passion is to encourage clients who get "Stuck" to take a deep breath in, hold it and then exhale while saying "Up Until Now". In doing so, they release the shadows, gremlins, the whispers, and whatever else has been keeping them from moving forward. By giving themselves permission to release all of the past — they can focus on being fully present "in the moment", to enjoy each day and look to the future they choose.

What will it take for YOU to step into a journey of releasing the past, enjoying the present and creating the future you desire?

Contact

Website: www.lilalarsoninternational.com
Email: coachinglinks1@gmail.com

Legacy of Love and Joy

By Lila Larson

"Life is meant to be a dance for joy!"

— Matthew Kelly

Have you ever wondered what it would be like to experience unconditional love and support?

I have been blessed with that experience for many years and am grateful to have learned what that felt like.

My parents, Bill and Florence Davis, and my Aunt Marguerite Schumacher were my 'Prayer Warriors' who gave me unconditional love and support as long as they lived.

What does unconditional love from a 'Prayer Warriors' feel like?

Let me share some ways that I experienced their love and support and that brought me joy.

I first got measles at age five and was confined to my bedroom with the shades pulled down to protect my eyes from the sunshine as that was the practice then. I peeked through the corner of the blind when I heard a yipping sound. There was a tiny puppy running around in the front yard. I said, "Wow! It's a puppy!" My aunt had taken the bus to our small town carrying the puppy in her coat, as dogs were not allowed on the bus. She wanted me to have something to look forward to when I could get out of my quarantined bedroom. I was so excited that I was going to be able to play with my new puppy that I agreed to stay in my dark bedroom until the time when I could get out.

My aunt always seemed to know what I would like and treasure. When I entered the 7th grade, which was close to my birthday, she gave me a black mock turtleneck sweater set. With my red hair, newly shorn for entry to middle school, the contrast was dramatic and daring for a teenager in those days. I was convinced that I was very grown up and gratefully thanked her. I still have the pearl collar that I wore with that sweater set so many years ago.

When I entered the 9th grade, she gave me a 2-piece outfit; a grey straight skirt with a kick pleat in the back and a matching fitted vest with red and white piping. Was I ever proud to be wearing such a sophisticated set. No one in the whole school had such an outfit. How she ever knew what would be valued by a new teen I will never know.

These are some examples of the unconditional love I received from one of my 'Prayer Warriors'.

My parents provided so many opportunities for me to experience their unconditional love over the years.

We used to accompany my parents when they went to visit friends, family, and members of Dad's congregation as we didn't have babysitters in those days. On one of those trips, I fell asleep in the back seat. When I woke up, I didn't know where everyone was, and I didn't recognize the house, the walkway or the yard. I was crying as I knelt on the floor of the back seat because I felt so alone and frightened. Then I heard voices and Mom and Dad were running to the car as they heard me crying. They scooped me into their arms and reassured me that they had NOT left me, only that they didn't want to disturb me as I was sleeping so peacefully. What reassurance I felt, knowing that I was loved and that they wanted me to rest. They never left me alone in the car again if I fell asleep. I was awakened and went with them.

Another opportunity arose when I wanted to find work at a summer resort where the family had a cottage. What it meant was that Mom and us three kids moved to the beach for the summer and Dad came out on the weekends when he wasn't preaching somewhere. This made it possible for me to get a job, even though I was only 14, and earn some money to buy fabric and make some of my own clothes.

What was the most memorable opportunity where I felt their loving support was when I wanted to go to Wales with a Schola Cantorum Choir from my high school to compete in an International Eistedford in LLanghollen Wales. I was to finish high school in June and the trip was to happen in July. I needed to pay for the air fare, billeting in Wales, the hotel and breakfast in London, lunch and supper, coins to pay for the electric meter in the bedroom, sightseeing in London, buying milk, buns, cheese, and olives from street vendors. Where was I ever going to get the funds?

Mom and Dad loaned me the funds to prepay the trip, with the promise that upon return I would work the rest of the summer and pay them back before September. I promised and I did. I was motivated to keep my promise in appreciation for their trust in me that I would keep my word and allow me to experience such a fabulous trip. I felt their love and support once again.

I learned the value of making and keeping a promise, the importance of personal integrity, and that keeping one's word is what defines a person's character and demonstrates and individual's worth.

Oh, how excited I felt sitting on a plane for the very first time with 65 other choir members and chaperones. After a long flight from Winnipeg to Manchester, England, we were bused to LLanghollen, Wales where we were billeted out in nearby towns during the festival. We had to guard the bathroom door for each other as there was no lock on it and we ate lunches in our room.

I still remember seeing and being repelled by the scrambled eggs being served in the morning after the cross Atlantic flight where the eggs had turned yellow because they had been sitting in grease since Winnipeg. It was many years before I could eat scrambled eggs again without seeing the orange-colored mess floating in grease and the scent which was appallingly undesirable as breakfast.

What I learned about joy on that trip was that the camaraderie of school chums focused on singing our hearts out together; chatting with members of other choirs from across Europe; sharing meals in the dining tent for lunch and evening meals; opened my eyes to what we did differently, and how what we were doing brought us into the finals. I was excited to use high school French to communicate with other attendees from France, Spain, Italy (and was thrilled when I was understood). Our accomplishments were rewarded with trophies in each of the three categories we had entered. What a thrill! The trip home was filled with stories of our individual encounters with members from other countries.

By focusing on why we were there and supporting each other every day — we were excited to be part of an International community where life was filled with exciting competitions, events where we met new people, and shared with each other the joy of being together in a new country.

Joy is possible wherever we are and in whatever circumstances we are in. It is a choice we make every day. Choose joy for yourself! Life is to be lived with anticipation, excitement and gratitude.

Mom and Dad were also encouraging as I tossed around options for what I would do after high school. One day, while eating in my school classroom, I tossed a coin. Heads up — teaching; Tails — university nursing program. It came up tails, which resulted in another toss. Mom was a nurse and so was my aunt. It was a decision point. University and nursing both required three years of education, but teacher training only required one year.

I had already borrowed money from my parents for the trip to Wales and if I enrolled in teacher training, I could live at home, which would save funds.

So, that was it. The decision was made. Mom and Dad remained committed to supporting me as I worked part-time while taking my training and helping out with my younger siblings and caring for my ailing grandparents who lived with us. Studying, helping with meals, laundry, cleaning, errands seemed such a small way for me to repay my parents for what they offered me on an ongoing basis.

What was an integral part of my growing up and into my adult years was the legacy of love, which was demonstrated through their actions and beliefs and allowed me to create joy in my life.

In addition, they (Mom, Dad, and my aunt) were 'Prayer Warriors' — every day of their lives. We began breakfast with Morning Devotions, began every meal with saying Grace... and prayed for family and friends regularly.

I learned what it was to be observant about what was needed by others, to listen for what was said and could be provided by any of us to make their lives easier and more comfortable.

There was never a question that if a family member needed to be in the city for medical treatment, that they would stay with us. That meant staying in my room as I had a single and a double bed. If treatments were needed at home, Mom would provide, and Dad would drive them to and from the doctor or hospital as needed.

How all of this was done on a limited salary, with 4 kids, and Mom still recovering from polio and learning to walk again I marvel yet.

Dad displayed his love for Mom in so many ways. He turned the main floor pantry into a bathroom with a toilet, sink, tub and shower so that she didn't have to go upstairs as she was learning to walk again. He turned the downstairs dining room into a bedroom for her so she could remain on the main floor. I saw him lifting and carrying things for her as she couldn't hold on to the wall and walk and carry things at the same time.

How have these examples and lessons affected me in bringing joy into my life?

Their willingness to make sacrifices and teach me by example how to sacrifice, demonstrated an incredible depth of love that I could then share with family, friends, coworkers, and future clients.

I have chosen to share what I learned from their legacy of love in my own life, and in so doing, I create joy each day. And as I have created joy in my own life, I have been able to encourage and support others to create joy in their lives.

I've also learned that life is what you make it. It's not which way the wind blows, it's how you set your sails. There was always music, laughter, and joy in our house and yard as we treasured times together with both immediate and extended family gatherings.

The joy came with oodles of photos and created memories that I fondly reflect on as I sort through them. I am grateful that I had the 'Prayer Warriors' in my life as long as I did.

After 70 years together, Mom and Dad died only 11 weeks apart to the day. Mom, age 95, died of a broken heart after Dad, age 94, passed away. My aunt died one year later at age 93.

They continued their commitment as 'Prayer Warriors' to the day they died, and I was blessed to be at their sides holding their hands.

They are always with me!

What joy I have in my heart to have been given such wonderful opportunities and experiences to recall and photos to look back on, and the lessons I learned from them about what life is for us.

When you choose to create joy in YOUR life, you are able to share that joy with others and feel happier, more appreciated and valued.

Always remember . . . you are creating the legacy of joy, peace and love in your life. 🏵

My Aunt Marguerite   My Parents, Bill and Florence Davis

Notes

Dr. Alice Cheung

A lice is a dedicated and professional educator for thirty years. She works with educational organisations and awesome people to bring inspirations and transformative enhancement to their lives, helping them uncover possibilities, advance in careers, and build dream relationships.

As an Amazon bestselling author of *The Purpose*, a contributing author of *The Book on Joy* in 2021, Speaker, Trainer of The Success Principles and Canfield Methodology, and Success Coach, Alice provides step-by-step guidance to help people achieve great success in three months, *Design Your Success*.

Her passion for education and extraordinary story of transforming her own life from "zero, low self-esteem" to "hero, confident" has aspired Alice to providing invaluable service, with a sound curriculum, to kids and their parents in family leadership in international landscapes.

Alice enjoys life with her amazing husband and two incredible children in Hong Kong. She loves hiking, traveling and sharing her expertise with friends to help them succeed in life.

Contact

Email: alicethepurpose@gmail.com

Evolving in the Joy of Learning

By Dr. Alice Cheung

"The most beautiful thing in the world is, precisely, the conjunction of learning and inspiration. Oh, the passion for research and the joy of discovery!"

— Wanda Landowska

I started school later than my age group because of poverty. My adoptive mom struggled to make ends meet. There were only the two of us. As a single mom, she did her best to provide a good living for me despite the frustrations and challenges encountered. I was eight years old when I started school. In Hong Kong, kids usually go to Kindergarten at the age of three, and then begin their Primary one (Grade one) at six. I joined other kids in a Primary two class without any prior schooling.

Daily, I ran home crying during those early school days because I loathed being called "Zero-egg," depicting I got zero marks. I felt like my heart was pierced when those words stung me. I was continually fighting back tears and wished I could escape and drop out. I was distraught. I did not blame my classmates as I consistently scored poorly, or no mark in my English. Those school days were painful to live until one day . . .

Ms. Ho, my English teacher, came to my rescue.

I still remember how I absorbed her words like a sponge.

She said, "I will teach you the English alphabet every day. Use this copybook to practice writing and learn the individual letters and sounds one by one. You need to remember everything I teach you!"

I declared, "I can't learn English. It's too hard."

"Of course, you can learn English! Drop the words 'I can't' from now on!" exclaimed Ms. Ho.

Taking Ms. Ho's advice, I persistently practiced English with my heart and my soul. If there were two big days in my life, I would say one is my birthday and the other one is the day that Ms. Ho announced my English test results. I was thrilled by Ms. Ho's words, "Class, I am so happy and proud of all of you. The whole class passed the English dictation. No one failed. Not anyone!"

"Including me??" I questioned my teacher.

"Of course, dear!" Ms. Ho reacted in no time.

"Joy is what happens to us when we allow ourselves to recognize how good things really are." — Marianne Williamson

That was the first time I found joy in learning. No more "Zero-egg!" I was excited, as tears were streaming down my cheeks. Without a cue, my classmates stood up and applauded. Then some ran to me with hugs. I felt like I had landed on the moon, where I was weightless and floating. Starting from that moment, I knew I could learn English, and I could learn anything. Everyone learns, but not at the same pace. Teachers should instill this concept in students and remind them not to give up. Nevertheless, the effort pays off, and persistence is the key to learning anything successfully. That is the joy of learning.

Poverty never left mom and me. Yet, having experienced the joy of learning, I insisted on continuing my study at school by exploring different means to overcome the dropout risk due to poverty. I stayed in my teacher's home and helped them with house chores, I served as a private tutor to help school kids with their English, and I worked in a factory during summer break to help relieve my mom's financial burden. Hardships never stopped me from continuing my study at school. I loved the joy of success in learning, as it made me stronger.

Over the years, I developed a high motivation for learning, as it was joyful for me to gain new knowledge and become a better "version" of myself. My teachers inspired me to pursue my training to become an English teacher. I entered one of the colleges for teacher training in Hong Kong after graduating from secondary (High) school.

During my college years, I was elected as the student union president, working together with 13 other members, including Paulus, who later became my incredible husband. I seized every opportunity to learn and grow by planning, organizing, and implementing student activities to enrich fellow students' lives. I was grateful for the opportunity to practice leadership, negotiations, communication skills, conflict resolution, and handling student complaints. These experiences built a solid foundation for me to excel and thrive in my future workplace.

At the age of 22, I started teaching English. I thought I was not good enough. I always wanted to improve myself. I set a plan to further study in the United Kingdom (UK) by earning a Bachelor of Education degree specializing in teaching English to speakers of other languages. I achieved this goal by saving most of my monthly salary and only spending money on essential needs. In the UK, I put my heart and soul into learning and practicing English as I did in my early school days. I learned about English culture and traditions using every opportunity to learn and interact with native speakers. It was an enjoyable learning experience for me.

After returning to Hong Kong to continue my teaching, I shared my experiences from the UK with my colleagues and students. My colleagues told me that I became more enthusiastic and passionate when teaching my lessons. If you treat teaching as a work of the heart, you will have great joy in bringing learning into learners' hearts.

Learning empowers and brings joy to others.

I continued to learn by earning a Master's degree in teaching English as a second language. Then, I began to teach in a vocational training school, which provides job-related training for students aged from 15 to 20. These students lacked an English language foundation and are of low motivation for learning English. It seemed like we were very distant. Learning English was joyful to me, but painful for them. I was determined to help them find joy in learning.

Thinking of how Ms. Ho helped me in my journey of learning from "zero" to "hero," I was determined not to give up on these students.

Instead, I wanted to find out why they were in a "frozen" mode in learning English when they joined the school. I was wondering if they had a similarly poor experience as I had before. I was determined to be a teacher who gave them hope. I was frustrated when I volunteered the kind of help that Ms. Ho gave me. It just didn't work! They didn't want to learn at all. Most of them had a rooted belief that "I can't" learn English. It was a big puzzle to me as I told them to drop the words "I can't" and replace them with "I can learn English" and "I will learn English." I concluded that there must be something wrong in their past experiences. I wanted to re-wire the joy of learning into the heart of these students. I continually worked to improve the situation.

During the next ten years of experimenting, I could not find the answer. I enrolled in a doctoral degree program to conduct deep and sensitive research to find out why they didn't want to learn English. It was not a straight road at all. I got rejected by 180 students when I invited them to join the research. I understood more as I got rejected more. I suspected that there definitely must be something painful with the students' past experiences. Then, I was inspired to work with non-English teachers who also had a negative attitude towards learning English. Finally, I got four teachers who agreed to be interviewed. I was shocked when they revealed their experiences. For example, driven out of the house for not paying attention to homework, being humiliated in front of the whole class for direct copying from a book, assignment got torn and thrown out of the window for not being attentive in class, and being marginalized because of her Chinese accent. What I have learned is that everyone has a unique background story.

Experiences grow out of other experiences. What children experience in their early life would be a memory for their future growth. The memory can enhance or hamper their personal and professional development. Teachers and parents can have a lasting influence on a child's life that may be difficult to erase.

When I look back on what I have learned, I feel grateful for all the opportunities I have had. Living in poverty is not all bad. The difficulties in my childhood make me treasure what I missed in life. I have learned to be grateful in life, especially to those who have helped me. Ms. Ho's patient teaching inspired me to the habit of "practice makes progress." I will not give up easily when I encounter difficulties in life. I will also extend Ms. Ho's passion to my students who are in need. Learning to overcome difficulties is a joy to me.

Now in my life, I firmly believe that learning is growing. Growing in knowledge makes a person become a better person. With this in mind, my husband and I always strive to stimulate our children's interest in learning. We made every effort to provide them with the best possible environment to learn and grow. When they were young, we bought them storybooks and read with them every night before putting them to bed. We also participated in the school's activities to learn and grow as parents. For example, we attended parents' talks and parent-child activities for relationship building. We also joined the school's reading program to cultivate a reading habit in our kids. I even volunteered to go to their school to be a storyteller for their classmates. Our two children, Lok and Yan, have developed their love for reading with all our efforts. We are gratified that they have joy in learning since their early days of reading.

I believe we have passed the joy of learning onto our children, and they will continue to give this as a gift to our grandchildren and the people around them.

Believing in the beauty of learning, I will grasp every opportunity to learn and grow. I know my growth and improvement will contribute to a more beautiful world.

Two recent accomplishments for me are my certification as a Canfield Methodology Trainer and writing my first book, *The Purpose*. I wrote this book to encourage people to persistently keep going in the face of difficulties and make their dreams come true. Without having a learning and growing mind, this book would not have been possible.

The ability to learn, write, and publish a book in English is joyful to me.

Learning makes me grow, growing makes me strong, strength gives me energy and courage to rise to challenges in life, making a better version of myself. Overcoming challenges helps me gain success. In learning to become a trainer for *The Success Principles*, I had the courage to do Facebook Live and become aware that "I am enough" and "I have worth." Remember, you and everyone can learn, grow and inspire others, thus contributing joy to the world.

"Whatever your mind can conceive and believe, it can achieve."
—Napoleon Hill

Debbie Prinster

❀

D ebbie Prinster was born in Los Angeles and attended schools in La Crescenta, California. She graduated from Brigham Young University with honors and her degree in elementary education. She taught Kindergarten through 5th grade even teaching online Kindergarten during the Covid pandemic. Debbie continues to work in the field of education while managing her Young Living Essential Oils business.

Debbie lives with her husband and four children ages 14 to 20 in Highland, Utah. She loves getting involved in her community, church and meeting her neighbors as she has lived in many states including: California, Nebraska, Nevada, Georgia, Pennsylvania, and Utah.

Failed Batches

By Debbie Prinster

"Everything Beautiful in Its Time"

—Jenna Bush Hager

Strawberry freezer jam brings me joy! I love spreading it on buttered toast and buttered rolls. I love it with whipped cream on pancakes and French toast. My husband loves it, and my children love it too. I look forward to this summertime tradition, that continually brings me joy!

Some years past, my family picked the strawberries straight from the strawberry plants at a nearby farm for the freezer jam, and other years, I have bought the strawberries from the grocery store. As long as I follow the directions exactly as written, the jam is always amazing. One year, I missed a step in the process, and the end result was not enjoyable or edible.

Every year since then, I have worked carefully step-by-step until the jam is safely in the freezer and I can breathe a sigh of relief. I could have given up after that first failed batch, but I love freezer jam, and I was not willing to give up. Life is full of "failed batches," and yet I find joy in second attempts and successes.

Besides freezer jam . . . chocolate chip cookies bring me joy!

After my husband's job transfer last year and our subsequent move, I made my first batch of chocolate chip cookies in our new home, in our new state. Unfortunately, my usually yummy, fluffy cookies were completely flat and crispy. After a few more "failed batches," I knew something was wrong. I started asking questions and discovered that since our new home was located in a high altitude area, I would need to add a little extra flour to my recipe. Turns out, that is exactly what my recipe needed, just a little extra flour. The next batch was deliciously wonderful, and I found joy in that attempt and the success that followed.

Both of these experiences remind me of the spider that we sang about in my Kindergarten class. I loved to sing "The Itsy, Bitsy Spider" with my students. After the spider is washed away in the middle of the song, the sun comes out, and the spider goes up the waterspout again. Getting washed off the waterspout is a "failed batch," but the spider doesn't let that get in the way. As soon as the sun comes out and the rain dries, the spider is onto that second attempt.

We had fun with the song and the actions in class, but more important to me was the message of "Try, Try Again."

Unfortunately, today's generation is struggling with the "Try, Try Again."

I attended a parent-teacher meeting at the beginning of the school year where my daughter's English teacher shared an interesting graphic. There were two pictures side by side, each denoting a path to success. One was a straight shot to success and the other was a windy road, like Lombard Street in San Francisco, with success at the end. The teacher said that the winding road was the actual path to success...with setbacks and twists along the way. I realized later why she shared this comparison . . . kids today aren't used to failing.

Most want the quickest and easiest path to success. And if it looks like failure is involved in the process, they'd rather avoid the path. They don't want to have any "failed batches."

We used to (and still do) have 'helicopter moms', but now there is a new term . . . the 'snowplow parents.' These are the parents that are going out in front of their kids, removing obstacles to ensure their kids succeed . . . and prevent them from failing. But, failure is a learned experience. By removing the possibility of failure, parents also prevent kids from learning that failure is a part of life and developing valuable coping skills, such as getting knocked down, learning a lesson, and then course correcting by thinking, "How can I do it differently next time?"

Today's generation is afraid of failure . . . afraid of a "failed batch." So, they try to avoid it.

Which means they often don't 'go for something' unless they feel like they can do it perfectly. They want to win every time. But that's not life. They are missing opportunities in life, such as taking up a new skill, or navigating a room full of strangers.

This idea is summed up in an article from Inc. Magazine, stating, "They've grown up in a connected world where failure is more public and permanent. One wrong move and the Internet can immortalize one's failure. In addition, success is prioritized over failure on social media. Millennials don't see the missteps of their friends on social media, which gives the false illusion that they are the only one experiencing failure."

The article continues, "According to a Babson College survey, 41 percent of 25-34-year-old Millennials cited "fear of failure" as their biggest roadblock to starting a business, up from 24 percent in 2001. It would seem that Millennials are searching for safer paths toward success . . . Now Millennials are entering the workplace where some are experiencing failure for the very first time, and it's up to managers to help them thrive through it."*

We need to teach kids that it's OK to fail...that it's part of life. The only way to do that is let them fail sometimes. If you have children, you know that one of the most difficult things to do is to allow your child to fail.

My sister told me about a situation when her daughter was in a 9th grade Honors English class. The teacher held high expectations and required students to read a minimum number of books during the semester. Although my sister constantly reminded (nagged) her daughter about the reading requirement, she didn't complete the assigned reading. At the end of the semester, her daughter assumed that she would sign the reading log, even though her daughter didn't complete the reading. The hardest thing for my sister to do was to not sign the log, knowing that her daughter's grade would drop, lowering her high school GPA with ensuing consequences.

---

*https://www.inc.com/ryan-jenkins/how-to-help-millennials-overcome-failure.html

Failure is a learned experience. As parents, one of the greatest gifts we can give our kids (and ourselves) is to be able to see the positive lessons after "failed batches."

I love the Special Olympics theme: "Let me win, but if I cannot win, let me be brave in the attempt."

If we teach our children that failure is OK, that it's simply part of the process . . . we are also teaching them to feel the joy of success. We don't fully feel success unless we've known failure. So, though it seems counterintuitive, one way we can share joy with our kids is allowing them to fail.

We can teach by example...going for things and being willing to fail. It's important for our children to see us deal with failure in a healthy way.

When I was in high school, I tried out for the senior cheerleading squad, but didn't make it. I was devastated. I put everything I had into the audition and wanted it desperately, but it didn't work out. What happens when we face these types of setbacks. Thankfully, my mom always had the attitude that something better was always out there — that you could find joy in many different things. I ended up running for senior class president and won! It was a long shot, but it worked out. I was really glad I didn't let the first failure keep me from putting myself out there again.

In terms of the spider song, we will wait for the sun to come out and the rain to dry, and then we will climb the waterspout again.

Not all of life's "failed batches" can be corrected by following the directions more closely or adding a little flour. Some "failed batches" are not based on our personal decisions or actions, they are directly or indirectly related to the decisions and actions of others. When the "failed batch" is something that we can control, then that is what we will do. We can control our attitude, our effort, and our dedication, and those "failed batches" can lead us to opportunities, learning, and self-reflection. For those other "failed batches" in life that are out of our control, we make the best of it and continue forward.

In life, rain will come, but amazingly enough, the sun will come again too. It is challenging to get back up after getting washed away, but we can find confidence, inspiration and joy in the second, third, and fourth attempts, and the successes that will follow. ✿

Notes

Lorna Granger

❃

Compassion, Caring and Service is what sparks every part of Lorna in her career as a Nursing Attendant, Mindset Coach and all round positive human being in the best way she knows how.

Within her career and life experiences, she discovered her gentleness, kindness and caring heart . . . Allowing her teachings of life to guide her and allow her to be herself.

She is grateful and honoured to be part of the healing of those who have invited her into their journey of life. Being able to share love, compassion, and caring through support is a true gift.

For the last 15 years her focus on supporting others deepened with tools of transformation to help them believe in themselves, connect to their inner gifts of purpose, embrace their beauty through authenticity and share it with the world.

This is her Joy and Love for Life.

Working from the Inside Out

Contact
Email: granger99@gmail.com

My Joy and Love for Life

By Lorna Granger

*"When you change the way you look at things,
the things you look at change."*

— Wayne Dyer

As a small child, every moment is an adventure, exploring the new with an openness, no attachments, allowing, acknowledging, learning and growing.

The river of life flows to us and through us, when we allow it. Sometimes fast and rough,' sometimes calm and gentle. Every part of the flow builds us in our purpose. It sparks us, opening our heart to giving and receiving love - the Joy in life.

Are all our moments filled with Joy?

No. Why?

Sometimes those fast-swift rough waters, bring other "gifts" that leaves one feeling sad, fearful, or maybe angry. We fight to find the goodness. We push against the flow trying to stop it, or drown those feelings, pushing them down deep, hoping they will never surface.

This challenging flow has a message for us. It bears a "gift" in life learning. Choosing to remember the child within us, we grow as we allow, acknowledge, learn, and let our feelings surface. We give them voice and unwrap the gift, as we become aware of the hidden goodness inside. This calms the flow and gentles our heart centre and opens it to joy.

Finding the Joy and Love in the Experiences

"I woke the morning after my husband passed away with intense pain in my body and the voice of a crying little girl in my head repeating over and over, "Who will take care of me now?"

Tightly curled in a fetal position, that was creating pain in every muscle of my body and a little girl's voice throbbing in my ears, as she was begging me to listen. That's when I realized the little girl was me at age three. That's how old I was when my mom passed away, and my dad chose alcohol to numb his heartache of sadness. He later succumbed to this illness.

In the current moment, I heard myself reply to the 3-year-old me: I AM, I AM. As I continued repeating "I AM," I could feel the muscles in my body let go and my 3-year-old's voice faded away as I said, "Take my hand, we will walk together, everything is going to be okay."

That was the day I chose to take responsibility for my life, my feelings and the emotions they created.

Most of my life I lived around a belief that someone needed to look after me and love me. Even as I got older this unconscious belief was confirmed for me in so many ways. I allowed others to think for me, speak for me and do for me. That usually didn't feel good, but I didn't understand then why I allowed it. It took a few life experiences for me to realize my past reactions allowed me to drown the pain of my mom passing and my dad choosing alcohol.

That day I knew I didn't want to walk a similar path as my dad and that if things in my life were going to change, I needed to take charge. I gave myself permission to acknowledge my pains, give them voice through acceptance, forgiveness, and self-love. This process of allowing the learnings to open my heart and inspired me to find the Joy in the gifts they delivered.

"When you change the way you look at things, the things you look at change." —Wayne Dyer

You see the one thing my husband of 30 years taught me from our life experiences was to believe in myself. I have the power to do anything I set my mind to do like giving and receiving love.

My mother gifted me life and love.

My father gifted me the awareness of choice and love.

In our time together the imprints they left on me, awakened me to self-love and the power of love.

The Spark Ignited

Life flows to us, when we live in the moment. We are in touch with the feelings within. The key is our awareness in the present and the emotions that are transported to us from life events. That awareness and how we choose to receive those feelings will determine the greater happiness, joy and love in our lives.

It took a few careers, considerable self-healing, taking responsibility for my life's choices, and learning to be present to my feelings. I gave myself permission to trust. That allowed the feelings to surface while opening my heart to receive the goodness that life was offering me.

Life was offering me my life's purpose.

Those feelings were inside me and embraced every part of me. They brought smiles to my heart and tingles to my feet like I was dancing to my favorite song. I connected with them immediately and that sparked my joy and love for life.

Remember . . . When you change the ways you look at things, the things you look at change.

In a blink of an eye, like a magic wand opening up my heart centre, I realized what others had been telling me about who I am for all these years. My passion and purpose presented in a way that stimulated every part of me from the inside out. I felt the Joy, the love, the wholeness in that spark.

It anchored itself with so much depth and clarity it was easily felt in every cell of my being. I knew then, what they had all been trying to tell me, about me, all this time. People could see it in me, it wasn't until I felt it, I knew. People can share much with us, about us, it's only when we awaken ourselves in being open to all, we arouse our inner gifts, our authenticity, our purpose.

My current career is where that anchor landed that brought full attention to my purpose, that had been growing steadily within me. My uniqueness, no other like me and the way I delivered it to others. It was in a setting that taught me that giving is the gift to receiving. Oh, the Joy and Love it's print leaves.

As a nurse, a caregiver co-worker, friend, teacher, student, daughter, mother, and grandmother. I am honoured to share my gifts naturally with others.

This is my Purpose: Caring, Compassionate, Loving and Supporting.

This is my JOY and LOVE for Life. This is my purpose and I feel it in every part of my being when I am giving unconditionally, which opens my heart to receiving.

Holding the hand of a patient, allowing them voice, listening to their fears and worries and the gentle gesture, everything is going to be okay.

Most times all people want is someone to listen, and the softness in compassion and caring that gives them the feeling of comfort.

The fast-swift waters become calm and gentle again.

Love ignites calmness.

To be invited in and witness to this is an honour.

My Intention

As I live each Day may I make a difference and touch at least one heart . . .

Each day it is my gift to share smiles, love and joy with others organically."

Always for the highest good of all.

I am grateful for all who allow me to share my passion, purpose, love and Joy.

When you change the way you look at things, the fast and swift, becomes calm and gentle flows to and through with love.

We come into this world, in our own whole, perfect uniqueness, no other like us. The gift of life.

Our gift of life and purpose starts to become imprinted in each of us with every breath, every life experience. We have many teachers, many influences.

From our experiences we recognize what feels good and what doesn't.

When we feel good our whole is ignited and we naturally share our joys from the inside out.

Notes

Ilka V. Chavez

---❀---

I lka is a #1 international best selling author and a fervent leader with an extensive track record for helping individuals, communities and organizations reach their highest potential. She is a lover of people and life and is dedicated to mentoring and guiding people and organizations to identify and activate the leaders within. She is a strong believer that following God's design is the perfect blueprint for authentic leadership. Her goal is to awaken the masses and help them create and lead a life they love living everyday.

She is the President of Corporate GOLD LLC, a leadership consulting and coaching company. She is a certified emotional mastery, life mastery, and transformational executive coach, and an international inspirational speaker. She is passionate about leadership and leading in excellence. She has found joy in the journey of leading others and herself. Her slogan is "Learn It, Live It, Lead it!"

Contact

Websites: www.ilkavchavez.com and www.corporate-gold.com
Email: Ilka@corporate-gold.com

Joy is the Eternal Blessing in the Journey

By Ilka V. Chavez

"The joy in the journey is the blessing in disguise."

— Ilka V. Chavez

The search for joy is a constant state for many or a state of being to someone. Merriam Webster defines joy as, "The emotion evoked by well-being, success, or good fortune or by the prospect of possessing what one desires." It is sometimes defined as a state of happiness or felicity aka, bliss.

The only way to find true peace and joy is to stop fighting and let go. When my mother was young, she was bathing in a river when she started to get sucked into a hidden, deadly whirlpool. Not knowing how to swim, she simply froze in the water. Surprisingly, once the whirlpool dragged her down, it brought her right back up to the surface. It was because she didn't try to fight and swim out of it that she survived. I've never forgotten that lesson.

Besides my faith, I have always had three anchors in my life: My family, my health and my career.

All of a sudden, I found myself in a whirlpool in my own life. It was a tornado . . . a perfect storm. I was in the midst of what became a toxic marriage that was killing my mental health and self-esteem, not to mention damaging my amazing children. Unbeknownst to me, the rejection and Imposter Syndrome were plaguing my identity. At the same time, I was diagnosed with cancer and leading a demanding high-level team as the Chief of Operations of the National Vaccine Program Office in Washington D.C. I had also recently been elected to a local school board position.

I didn't know what to do. Should I fight to keep my family together? Should I fight for my health? Should I fight for my career? I realized I couldn't fight all three.

The more I fought and tried to escape the storm, the more exhausted, helpless and discouraged I felt. Quite frankly, fighting was killing me.

The doctor gave me three months off work and said, "You decide."

What I heard was, "You decide if you want to live or if you want to die."

I decided I wanted to live. I had to choose my mental and physical health.

In order to do that, I would have to follow my mother's example and stop fighting the storm. I gave up the dream of holding my family together, let go of my marriage and released that path to God, having faith that everything would be OK. I simply had to trust the process. I continued the important work of supporting my children during this difficult time, both mentally and emotionally. I stepped down from both my job and the coveted elected position, allowing the best path for me to emerge.

The decision to let go of what I thought were the pillars holding me together actually drew me to joy.

I was literally taken into the eye of the tornado and then released, coming to a place where I felt the deepest joy and peace I had ever known. Because even in the midst of the pain, I found joy and joy led me to peace.

And, indeed, everything did work out. In my family, my children and I remain close and I love them with all my heart. They bring me pure joy. Fortunately, in my career, others knew my value and supported me as I navigated through very tough decisions in my vocation. They helped me transfer to positions with lesser stress that could still capitalize on my strengths.

Neale Donald Walsch recently reminded me in one of his morning inspirations, "Safety is not the thing you should look for in the future. Joy is what you should look for. Security and joy may not come in the same package. They can . . . but they also cannot. There is no guarantee. If your primary concern is a guarantee of security, you may never experience the truest joys of life. This is not a suggestion that you become reckless, but it is an invitation to at least become daring." Imagine "Daring Joy". This inspirational message was so powerful and timely for me in this chapter of my life. I chose purpose over security, regardless of what others thought. I dared to be joy-filled, even though it made no sense for me to experience joy in this season.

Deciding for my purpose helped me experience complete joy. Through what I had faced, I finally gained a deeper understanding and feeling of joy. Oh, the blessing in disguise found in making the decision the soul desires, rather than the heart. This is limitless joy.

To experience joy in the journey you must expect it. "Expectation keeps your mind positive and your heart full. "For everyone who asks receives, and everyone who searches finds, and for everyone who knocks, the door will be opened." (Luke 11:10)

The blessing in disguise was that in pursuit of happiness, after my family, health and life as I knew it fell apart, I actually discovered joy. Joy and happiness are not the same. The missing link was joy and knowing that it was available to me regardless of my circumstances or conditions. I have learned that even during sad times, I could find the strength to rejoice. I could be sad and still feel joy. There was no need to limit my experience by just "happiness."

Joy is different from happiness. Happiness can be limiting and is not the ultimate destination on this journey. As explained by Desmond Tutu and the Dalai Lama: Happiness is limited as it is dependent on external sources. Without material things or people, it will not exist or remain as it relies on your senses and your emotion. Tutu continues, "Joy subsumes happiness." Once I understood and experienced joy over happiness, it became a game changer for me.

Additionally, it is important to understand that choosing joy is an intentional practice. It is anchored inside of you and no matter the external influences; you can feel it and experience it. Sometimes to find joy you just have to be still.

The courage to do things I never thought I could achieve was resurrected. Traveling solo, living solo, and enjoying my own company became common for me. I was operating differently as a woman, I handled life applications differently, I treated people with more love and care as they learned the truth I had found. I also realized that it takes a certain willingness to mature past the longings and discontents of the world to experience everlasting joy. What a revelation this was for me in my journey through life applications. The awakening of my soul and connection of my mind to soul were indescribable. I learned that I need not wait for short lived happiness as eternal joy is in me.

Lastly, finding joy allowed me to be more trusting and find peace when taking risks to strive for the greater good. These teachings, as I intimately discovered, allowed me to stand firm and love who I am, understand that I am enough for the right tribe, and to own and embrace my worth and truth.

I leave you with these thoughts as you continue to realize that joy in the journey is your blessing in disguise.

1. Do the work to free yourself from the limits the world places on you.
2. Pay attention: are you sad being by yourself and constantly need others to feel happy?
3. Note that joy is sometimes uncovered through pain and suffering.
4. Happiness is temporary, choose joy daily.
5. Forgive often
6. Give more
7. Love more
8. Serve more
9. Let gratitude reign in your life
10. Become intimate with and own who you are

I relate to Kay Warren who said, "Joy is the settled assurance that God is in control of all the details of my life, the quiet confidence that ultimately everything is going to be alright, and the determined choice to praise God in all things."

Seek wisdom from within and from others who have already found joy, to find your joy. There is liberty in finally learning that seeking happiness limits you, while seeking joy frees you. Rejoice in all things, persevere, and trust that it will all work out for your good.

Let go, be free, make the decision to experience pure joy.

Bernadette Ridge

❀

Bernadette is originally from Ireland and now lives on Spinnaker Island, close to Boston, Massachusetts. She is a former teacher with a B. Ed. Degree, a seasoned Workforce Engagement software solutions sales specialist, and her real passion is helping others and creating joy! She has achieved certifications in Strategic Intervention coaching, Miracle-Minded Coaching, Barrett Values System Leadership & Coaching, Jack Canfield/Kathleen Seeley Train-the-Trainer Virtual Skills, Applied Positive Psychology, amongst others. Through her leadership with a Boston organization committed to promoting the Irish language, she was included in a history book about people who made a difference between Connemara and Boston over the past 30 years. She is a member of the Healy World and Young Living organization, both complimentary to her mission. Bernadette has a huge appetite for life, a desire to create a legacy by helping others and making our world a more joyful place.

Contact
Websites: www.bernadetteridge.com and www.bridgeonjoy.com

Revelling in Joy

By Bernadette Ridge

"I have learned that people will forget what you said, people will forget about what you did, but people will never forget how you made them feel".

— Maya Angelou

I used to be the kind of person whose home, closets, and email folders — EVERYTHING — had to be perfect. I associated order and control with being responsible, secure and 'mature'. Even my fun was 'organized' for every Saturday night, and we rarely varied from the same theme.

I am smiling wryly as I think about my life today. I have definitely undergone a transformation!

These days, even living alone and working from home during the pandemic, I experience SO many incredibly joyful moments, that are mostly spontaneous. Random, but delightful text invitations, meeting new neighbours and friends, an unexpected invitation to ride a bicycle around Lebanon with 120+ women from 23 different countries, a sky-dive adventure, going on a vegan themed cruise and a call to ask if I would consider collaborating in *The Book on Joy* . . . Yes! Yes! Yes!

I live by a few guiding principles that work well for my life, i.e. Never put 'things-to-do' before people and say YES to everything (within reason!). Sometimes I wonder what great adventures I missed out on in my earlier years by being the responsible 'good girl'.

In hindsight, it all makes perfect sense. I am the eldest daughter of seven children born to my amazing parents, who were also our teachers, in a two-teacher school. Think about that, for a moment! We lived in rural Ireland — a magical, beloved place called Connemara on the west coast of Galway. I was also the eldest of more than 50 cousins on my dad's side. What a treat they all are!

As I think back to my formative years, those years where our human conditioning seems to be our 'defining time', I remember feeling like a 'mis-fit'. I was caught somewhere between being the eldest child with responsibilities beyond my years, the teacher's daughter at school, and at home, I was the sister who behaved more like a parent. To grow up in a relatively small home, full of people with secrets and stories, I some-how never felt 'in the middle of it'. I often felt lonely. But my instinct reassured me I would find my place in the world eventually.

At 17, I met the man who would become my first husband and we were together for almost 25 years. He was very ill for a long time, resulting in my leaving my teaching job in Dublin and moving to London, where he had his last, successful operation. I was working three jobs to make ends meet in those early days when other teenagers were having the time of their lives.

And then — the joyful MIRACLE! A totally unexpected call one Tuesday night from the U.S. division of my company asking if I would consid-er coming to the U.S. for two years. That would be my first and most significant, spontaneous, joyful decision! I could hardly believe how easy it was to give up my marriage, my "perfect home", friends, family, EVERYTHING — and move to Boston, USA, a city I had never even visit-ed before. It was a whirlwind three months organizing L1 visa, initiating divorce, selling our home and furniture, yet I was on fire and ready for my new adventure.

As the poem, "For a new beginning" says, "Awaken your spirit to ad-venture. Hold nothing back; learn to find ease in risk. Soon you will be home in a new rhythm. For your soul senses the world that awaits you." —John O'Donohue 'Benedictus'

Every day was a new adventure and I was thrilled. But those nights on my own, looking out at Boston Harbour, were lonely. I was 42 years old, knew no one in Boston besides new work colleagues and that freedom I craved was not as easy as I anticipated. Who was I now, after all? One night, I discovered the miracle of Leonard Cohen's music and poetry, including the quote that hangs on a wall opposite my bed to this day:

"Ring the bells that still can ring, forget your perfect offering, there's a crack in everything, that's how the light gets in." —Leonard Cohen

That mind-shift caused me to make the second most significant, spontaneous, joyful decision, to figure out what my 'cracks' were and how they might serve me in letting light in. I then began a self-discovery journey that will likely never end. I said YES to everything and worked with Landmark Education, Jack Canfield, Mary Morrissey, Mark & Magali Peysha, Linda Jones, The Flourishing Center, Mike Dooley, Kathleen Seeley, Marianne Williamson — to name but a few. This education has been invaluable, especially in helping me through times where definite cracks showed up in my life, including my mom's death, my brother's suicide, four cousins' suicides, two divorces, job losses, broken body parts, etc.

The more I learned about mindset (how thoughts becoming things), my willingness to see things differently, such as the number of people in unnecessary pain, my capacity for love, empathy, fun, positivity, and sheer joy went through the roof! The ringtone on my cell-phone is Pharrell Williams' "Because I'm happy" song, and I love it.

I realized I am happiest when I am with people, laughing, dancing, having deep conversations and just being totally present in the moment.

I found my deepest spirituality and realized I am not the architect of my life, merely the builder. Whether we call it God, Spirit, Intuition or Instinct, the alignment of mind and soul creates peace, which is the platform for true joy. I believe that, at their peak, religion and psychotherapy are the same thing — paths to healing the mind.

Leaving a legacy has always been important to me. I have not been blessed with children but I realize that also was part of the divine architecture of my life. I am free to give of my time, energy and love to others, including some amazing children around the world.

My passion truly is to serve others and I am blessed that my sales career is aligned with this. As a miracle-minded coach, positive psychology practitioner and one of the happiest people on the planet, I am committed to helping others, to making people I engage with feel happy, care-free, understood, appreciated and loved — even if just for the moments of brief encounter.

I smile as I recall a recent moment at my favourite Boston Irish bar — Mr. Dooleys. I was there with my second ex-husband and a group of dear friends (The Shenanigators), and it was the first night of live music without masks or restrictions. The energy was magical! When one of my favourite songs — The Galway Girl — started, I got up to dance. Out of nowhere, a young Japanese guy literally leapt onto the dance floor, arms and legs wildly flailing, the biggest grin on his face — pure JOY! My friends left us to it and recorded the moment for posterity. After the song ended, we had a big hug and a baby Guinness shot together. Within minutes, the dance floor was packed!

It is perhaps worth taking a moment to explain that there is an Irish word called 'shenanigans', which means 'silly or high-spirited behaviour; mischief'. I have different groups of friends and one of those I met during my Irish language teaching years, so we call ourselves 'The Shenanigators' and we even have T-shirts. Induction into this group is not for the faint of heart! I can't even begin to tell you how much joy this group creates, as well as how deeply they care for each other and fundraise for miraculous causes. Somehow, as I operate between these various groups, who have also, joyfully, become inter-mingled, I have earned the nickname 'Queen B'. It's a fun thing, but I am secretly quite proud of it! I have so much 'Queen B' paraphernalia now that it's ridiculous, but I know it's because I am loved, and people enjoy my company.

A miracle is a change in perception from fear to love. Miracles are born of conviction — a deep understanding that our purpose here is to co-create the healing of our world.

It is not up to me to decide what I learn but, what is ENTIRELY up to me (and you too, my friend!), is to learn through joy vs. pain. There are angels pushing us from behind if only we will let them, and just say YES! Be willing to see any situation differently, and it becomes different.

A Course on Miracles says: "I am the faucet, not the water". So let's let joy flow freely, spontaneously and revel in it. ✿

Notes

Cindy Stewart

———— ✿ ————

Originally from Northwestern Pennsylvania, then transplanted to Missouri, Texas and North Carolina, Cindy calls Kernersville "home". She is a Diploma RN (St. John's School of Nursing) followed by a BSN (Southwest Missouri State University); and a MBA/MHA Degree (Pfeiffer University). She is certified in Healthcare Quality, the Canfield Methodology and Train The Trainer Professional Development trainer. After 37 years in a variety of healthcare nursing roles, she decided to be her "own boss". As a successful business owner, she knows firsthand the impact joy has on lives.

An avid volunteer, she is involved with SistersHOPE.org, Kernersville Friends of the Library, Crisis Control Ministry, and the Kernersville Chamber of Commerce. Her words to live by are: FAITH, FAMILY (includes friends) and FUN.

Her purpose: encourage individuals to creatively DREAM BIGGER & DECIDE WHAT they want out of life!

Contact

Email: cindystewart250@gmail.com

Scatter Joy

By Cindy Stewart

"Scatter Joy"

— Ralph Waldo Emerson

Oh, how I would have loved meeting Ralph Waldo Emerson! To hear him speak and to be able to ask about the simplicity of his words, "Scatter Joy" would have been a gift. These words literally jumped out at me. In what I view as a very complex world, Emerson's words, evoke a strange feeling of simplicity. Curious as it may sound, how can life be so simple for one to scatter joy? Those two seemingly simple words made my imagination run wild with questions as to his meaning: 'Is the world simple, not complex? Is joy all around us? Why would he say such a thing? Can anyone scatter joy anywhere, anytime?'

Catching myself, I first settle in to ask, 'What elicits JOY and how can JOY be scattered?'

As I sat and pondered questions on this simple phrase, I came to understand joy is all around us. Joy has been with me my entire life. When I took a long, thoughtful look deep inside me, I found moments of joy have been scattered throughout my life. Joy is found in both the simple, ordinary times of life and in the extraordinary times. One might say that joy is an inner feeling that provides sheer delight and sheds light on our life's purpose or the purpose of a loved one. Family stories told throughout the generations reveal moments of joy.

I found there are many forms of joy as in simple joy, pure joy, tears of joy, songs of joy, life joy, and many more.

While pausing to figure out what Emerson meant by "Scatter Joy," I realized I am a natural scatterer of joy. It's in my blood from birth. I am a giver, a gifter, a volunteer and a servant leader. I've had these qualities as long as I can remember. I have always searched for the perfect gift to give family or friends that brings me joy like the perfect celebration card or notecard and attaching the ideal stamp prior to mailing. Discovering a new quote to use in my correspondence excites me and hopefully delights the receiver of the note. Simple pleasures bring me joy. Listening to a new song, reading a new book by my favorite author and exploring new shops is joyful for me. Being with family and friends and volunteering in the community for the American Red Cross, Crisis Control Ministry, The Friends of the Library, the Chamber of Commerce bring me joy. Joy is at the heart of my donating to those in need.

Allow me to scatter joy by sharing a few stories from my life told to me by my parents or from my own personal experiences. My father was an avid stamp collector. This was a hobby he started at an early age and continued throughout his entire life. My mother tells how my father on each payday would stop at the post office to buy a page of stamps, even when money was extremely tight. Although at the time buying stamps seemed to take priority over bill paying, my parents always seemed to manage. Even today, I visit the post office frequently to purchase stamps from animals to flowers to persons of interest in history. Although my stamp collection is not as impressive as my father's stamp collection, I scatter joy through handwritten notes using a personally selected stamp applied to each envelope.

Joy in ordinary times could be found in a smile. My father used to ask me to smile for him. I never quite understood why he asked this of me. I thought it was because I had straight front teeth, whereas, his were slightly overlapping. I could tell a smile from his children brought him joy. However, after having children of my own, I understood the value of a child's smile as one of those could brighten one's day and bring peace of mind.

Smiles were readily apparent during the holiday seasons in our home. Christmas time was always special for our family. Gathering together with family and friends, we could stay up a little later and sneak a few more treats. Holiday traditions of trimming the tree with bright colorful lights of red, blue, yellow and green; Christmas carols; Christmas cards; holiday open houses with friends and time with family. This was and is an easy way to scatter joy.

Then there are the stories mother shares of growing up in Pennsylvania with her best friend, (Shirley). At the age of five, they walked to kindergarten hand-in-hand. Even though it's been over eighty-five years, she vividly describes their walk to school and the excitement of school-life. Pure joy emerges as I witness my mother's face light up retelling this true tale. Another true tale of mother and her best friend (Shirley) happened during a visit to Michigan, where my mother, my older sister, and I made a visit to my mother's best friend and her husband, who was gravely ill. They had not seen each other in years. During our visit we heard stories of their days gone-by. We all laughed as we remembered some of those times when my parents had parties in our home while we were growing up. Within weeks after our visit, my mother's friend's son called us to let us know of recent death of his father, her best friend's husband. The son expressed how grateful they were for our visit and for the laughter we had brought into their home. His father could not stop talking about the "girls" sitting at the dining room table and laughing about such silly things from the past. Our visit scattered joy. Who knew?

For me, pure joy was witnessing the birth of a child. My introduction into childbirth was during nurses' training at the age of 18. I'll never forget the face of the father gazing in awe at his child. I was struck with such intense feelings that I wrote my mother a letter about the experience as soon as I returned to my dormitory room that evening. Later, I gave birth to children of my own. Two girls. The look on their father's face when he first held each of them in his arms is forever imprinted on my mind. I was transported back in time when I had written that note as a nursing student to my mother. Children have a natural way of sprinkling joy into our lives. Most recently, the birth of my first grandchild, Hadley May, reminded me how simple the birth of a child could miraculously scatter joy. Again, the look on a new father's face is unforgettable. To witness the wave of excitement as it spreads across the family as each member learns of the wonderful news of a new life. Scattering joy.

Joy in extraordinary times for me occur during celebrations of love, such as a wedding or during celebrations of life, such as graduations or funerals. While living in Austin Texas, I met the man who was the joy of my life, John Merryday Stewart. From the day we met, I knew we were going to be together. Surely, the look on our faces as a new bride and groom were captured after the wedding ceremony reflecting joy. In our family room today, I have such a photograph of John and me walking down the aisle of St. Joseph's Cathedral on a hot June day in 1980.

Joy radiates in love.

Another extraordinary time I recollect includes both my husband and his father. My father-in-law, the late Reverend J. Rufus Stewart, began each day bellowing out Psalm 118:24, "This is the day the Lord has made, let us rejoice and be glad in it". Even though twenty years have passed since he left the earth, I can still hear the sound of his deep southern voice and his commitment to his faith. Tears of joy.

Emerson knew what he was talking about. He was an insightful man. Joy is always with us. Whether it is the warmth of the sun, full moon at night, the gentle breeze on a scorching hot day, or simply the springtime green of trees in the neighborhood or park, JOY is simply everywhere for us to find.

How do I scatter joy? By being who I am. Being me to my family allows me to scatter joy through many roles as a daughter, sister, younger sister, older sister, granddaughter, grandmother, niece, cousin, wife, mother, aunt, and great aunt. Being me to my community allows me to scatter joy while serving others. Whether it is through a kind word, a smile, a simple "Hello, how do you do?" It is joy. Whenever I hear or use "How do you do?" I hear my Grandma Dickens speaking. No matter who she met, young or old, she always greeted each person with a solid, "How do you do?" My grandmother never met a stranger. To scatter joy in the community allows one to meet the individual person where they are.

Emerson believed in the individual. He wrote of individual joy. He knew joy is in each individual's heart, joy is in each individual's soul and joy is in each individual's spirit. He believed joy is constantly with us. Never are we without joy. We are JOY! "Scatter joy" clearly says it all. I scatter joy by being me. Giving. Gifting. Donating. Volunteering. Living.

How do **you** choose to SCATTER JOY? 🏵

Notes

Our Invitation to You

We honor you for investing in yourself by reading, sensing and engaging with us and our stories. We hope you feel connected and share our intention to make a difference in the world.

You can Join the 'Joy Journey' in several ways:

- Create more joy in your life, community or world. Tell us on our facebook page how you are doing that: www.facebook.com/thebookonjoy

- Write a chapter in one of our upcoming Inspired Life Series volumes.

- Learn how you can experience and inspire others with putting Joy Essential oil on your heart daily.

- Attend a virtual or live Inspired Joy Retreat

Stay in touch with our Team Joy at www.thebookonjoy.com.

Made in USA - North Chelmsford, MA
1290121_9780980110449
11 16 2021 0759